THE LIFE OF A MILITARY SPOUSE

YOUR DREAMS MATTER TOO

VIRGINIA BEACH, VA

Copyright © 2022 Kasey King, LMFT

All rights reserved. This document is geared towards providing exact and reliable information with regard to the topic and issue covered. The publication is sold with the idea that the publisher is not required to render accounting, officially permitted, or otherwise, qualified services. If advice is necessary, legal or professional, a practiced individual in the profession should be ordered.

No part of this publication may be reproduced, duplicated, distributed, or transmitted in any form or by any means, including photocopying, recording, or other electronic or mechanical methods, without the prior written permission of the publisher, except in the case of brief quotations embodied in critical reviews and certain other noncommercial uses permitted by copyright law. Recording of this publication is strictly prohibited and any storage of this document is not allowed unless with written permission from the publisher. All rights reserved.

The information provided herein is stated to be truthful and consistent, in that any liability, in terms of inattention or otherwise, by any usage or abuse of any policies, processes, or directions contained within is the solitary and utter responsibility of the recipient reader. Under no circumstances will any legal responsibility or blame be held against the publisher for any reparation, damages, or monetary loss due to the information herein, either directly or indirectly.

Respective authors own all copyrights not held by the publisher.

Printed by Kiyanni B., Write It Out Publishing, LLC. in the United States of America.

Write It Out Publishing LLC
Virginia Beach, Virginia
Writeitoutpublishing.com

ISBN: 979-8-9869842-4-7

Book Cover Illustrator: Maurice Rogers, Write It Out Publishing
Editor: Tamira Butler - Likely, Sheryl Johnson, Write It Out Publishing

First printing, (e-book & paperback) November 2022
Kasey King
Fort Worth, TX / info@ksalone.com

Featured Contributing Authors in this project maintain ownership of their writing material:
Leah Huggins | Shekendra Collins | Tajh- Marie Thompson

THE LIFE OF A MILITARY SPOUSE

YOUR DREAMS MATTER TOO

BY

KASEY S KING, LMFT

CO-AUTHORS

LEAH HUGGINS | SKEKENDRA COLLINS | TAJH-MARIE THOMPSON

DEDICATION

TO ALL MILITARY SPOUSES WHO FELT THEY HAD NO CHOICE. TO ALL THE SPOUSES WHO THOUGHT ABOUT GIVING UP. TO ALL THE SPOUSES WHO HAVE PUT THEIR COUNTRY AND THEIR FAMILY FIRST AND FORGET TO PUT THEMSELVES FIRST. THANK YOU FOR SHOWING UP DAILY WITHOUT COMPLAINT. THANK YOU FOR YOUR SACRIFICE. I APPRECIATE YOU. TO MY GRANDMOTHER, THE WOMAN I REFER TO WHEN I HAVE BEEN ASKED MY WHOLE LIFE WHO INSPIRES ME THE MOST. THE WOMAN I KNOW WORKED EVERY DAY IN A CAREER SHE LOVED AND WAS STILL AN AMAZING MOM AND WIFE. I HOPE I CAN CONTINUE TO MAKE YOU PROUD. I LOVE YOU. TO MY CHILDREN, THANK YOU FOR UNDERSTANDING THE WORK I DO AND SUPPORTING ME IN LIVING MY DREAMS. THANK YOU FOR THE SNACKS WHEN I WORK AND RANDOM HUGS. I HOPE I CAN BE AN INSPIRATION TO YOU. CHARLIE, THANK YOU FOR NEVER COMPLAINING, NEVER ASKING ME TO CHOOSE, AND FOR LITERALLY SUPPORTING EVERY CRAZY DREAM I HAVE.

I LOVE YOU.

CONTENTS

KASEY KING — 7

CHAPTER ONE — 9
I Never Really Wanted to Be Married...or Have Kids

CHAPTER TWO — 13
Life Before the Military

CHAPTER THREE — 17
I Am Not a Dependent

CHAPTER FOUR — 21
The Mistakes I Made

CHAPTER FIVE — 25
The Tried and ~~Failed~~ Unsuccessful Gigs

CHAPTER SIX — 31
Digging My Way Out of Depression

LEAH HUGGINS — 57

CHAPTER SEVEN — 59
A Bag of Her Own

SHEKENDRA COLLINS — 69

CHAPTER EIGHT — 71
My Name is SheKendra Collins

TAJH-MARIE THOMPSON — 113

CHAPTER NINE — 115
MEET TAJH

KASEY KING

KASEY KING

I am ready to divorce. I want to throw it all away. This is not what I thought it would be. I gave up so much, and what am I really getting in return? To travel from one city to the next is unstable and mentally exhausting as hell. Who in their right mind would want this life? Like, for real? I could have excelled so much higher had I not given up my dreams. Is that you?

At some point, we all may have said at least some of those statements. We all have wondered what our life would be like if. This is not saying we don't love our spouses, kids, and our annoying dogs. This is saying that you are human and you feel, you ponder, you grieve, and just get freaking tired once in a while. Sometimes you get so tired that you really want to be still and not travel with your spouse anymore. You really want to just stay where you are, let the kids finish school, and you stay at the great job you just found. I feel you on that and I have a story about it. But there is something in you, that spouse speaking, that spouse that reminds you of your other purpose, your other obligation to take charge of your family and to be available for when your soldier comes home from work, field exercise training, deployments, workups, etc. Then you snap back to reality, finish packing and leave for Pascagoula (yes, there is a base there). This is our life. It sucks. It can be depressing and so many other feelings that I cannot name. Maybe you can. Just insert those feelings here _____, here _____, and here _____. Oh, wait, don't forget about here _____. I knew you had one more.

Basically, you are the spouse of a soldier, and it doesn't get easy until it's over. However, while your solider is living their dreams, you can have your own too. The road will be tough and there will be some scarifies, which you will be no stranger to. Let's be honest, sacrifice should be our middle name, right? Kasey Sacrifice King. Yep, sounds like my life when I say it out loud. You should try it.

CHAPTER ONE

I NEVER REALLY WANTED TO BE MARRIED...OR HAVE KIDS

CHAPTER 1: I NEVER REALLY WANTED TO BE MARRIED...OR HAVE KIDS

Now, don't close the book. This is not a husband bashing, anti-marriage book, let me just put that out there. However, it was the truth. I was young, in the military, and living my life. It was a great life. I loved everything about being in the military for the first 7.5 years. Even though I was for sure getting out, this one officer solidified it for me (I will talk about him later). Now, I know I had my comment about crappy bases. To be completely fair, just as many outdated ones there are, there are also some extremely nice ones.

I loved being in San Diego in the early 2000s; it was my first duty station after Great Lakes. I met so many great people that are still doing their thing in the military today, or have just retired. In fact, had I stayed in, October 2022 would have been my 20 years. No thanks. I first met Evee, then Fletcher, Marshall, Brandy, Tiffany N., Tiffany J., and a couple of others were my day ones! Oh, Collins, TK, Reese, and the R division were my crew, you feel me!! I loved it! Monique and I were super tight. I was there when she delivered her baby, who just graduated high school this year. We were also roommates in our 600-sq-ft San Diego apartment and I loved it! I went from the ship in Mississippi, prior to arrival in San Diego, and we traveled through South America along the way. After my years in San Diego, I went to San Antonio, then Gulfport (where I met my husband), overseas to Bahrain, Jacksonville to process out, then back to Gulfport to the home we purchased. That is my 8.5 years in a paragraph. The military was great to me and in 2010, I was out.

The way my single life was set up (in my head), I was going to do one more tour, then move to Houston or San Antonio. I have yet to make it there, by the way, but we are in Texas. What I was going to do in those places, no clue, but I knew that was where I wanted to be. Then, I met my husband. Now, I know you may have a similar story. You were just minding your business, living your life and loving freedom, until someone appeared in your life that you were willing to relinquish (some of) that freedom for. I met someone in July 2005, shortly before my birthday, then hurricane Katrina. I was a Master At Arms (military police), so I knew everyone by cars. He had this dark red 1996 Cadillac Deville. He was so handsome, I had to tell my friend Angie who was right there working at the gate with me. We didn't talk then. It wasn't until weeks later in a club (don't judge me, I was only 21), that we officially met and talked. We military dated (long distance unofficially) and married in 2008. I would say the rest is history and it has been blissful since, but I would really be lying to you.

Since then, I have worked so hard at not using the word never. Never is the devil and always comes back to laugh at you. I can say with absolute assurance that my life did not go according to plan, but does it ever? I don't think I would have ever been able to come up with this version of my life on paper. I don't think I had the chance to reflect on the kids, animals, travels, jobs, friendships, and schools that led me here. There are things I would have changed, but nothing I regret and for that, I am able to lend my story to you in hopes that you are able to create the life of your dreams as a military spouse.

CHAPTER TWO

LIFE BEFORE THE MILITARY

CHAPTER 2: LIFE BEFORE THE MILITARY

I come from a family of military men. My great grandfather Sam was in WWII while serving in the Army. My uncle Sammie served in the Marine Corps during Desert Storm and his son served in the Army. I am the only lady in our family to serve. Some of my family were not happy about it, one being my mom. I believe she thought I would die. Looking back, I guess her feelings were justified since 9/11 was only a year prior. That was the most emotional I have ever seen her. I wasn't sure if there were more happy than sad, I just knew there were some of both. Prior to, I was in ROTC for three years and had been to three high schools. This year would be my 20th reunion, but I am not sure they would even remember me since I was only there for a year. I did not play any sports but loved them. My high school Algebra teacher always called me his center (he wanted me to play on the basketball team). I wanted to participate in many sports -but did none. If you ever watch sports with me, you will see my passion and think I played before. The only sport I played was soccer with a group of military spouses, while living in Virginia Beach. It was so much fun and one of the biggest things I did to serve one of my purposes as a spouse.

I was always a tall kid. I loved to read and to be outside. My favorite book was Charlotte's Web. Th movie was meh, but the book I still love to this day. Outside of that, I love going to the movie theatre. To this day, I am a movie buff. When I was single, a long time ago, I used to movie hop. If you don't know, movie hopping is when you go the movie theatre, watch one movie, then walk into another one. Don't try that these days, y'all. I don't think I am even that bold anymore. Life before the military was simple, as most things are when you are a kid. I grew up in Baton Rouge, Louisiana, and lived with my mama, grandmother, grandfather, and four other siblings. I am number two of five, but I am treated like I am number one (don't tell my sister). I don't have too many complaints about my early life, just one, but after reading Viola Davis,' Finding Me, you get no complaints from me. If you ever read her book or listened to the audible version (like me), then you know what I mean. My grandfather passed on Valentine's Day when I was twelve and my grandmother never remarried. My mama never married. I always wanted to be a nurse like my grandma. I don't even like hospitals, so later in life, I knew that was not even a possibility for me. Then, I thought I would be a teacher and would attend Southern Louisiana University (SLU) because everyone around that way went to Southern University and I just wanted to be different, even though Southern was the bomb. Whelp, I was different and went to the road less traveled (United States Navy). My good friend joined with me and flaked on me when it was time to officially be sworn in. I was hurt by that. I think I am starting to see the pattern of **my plans don't go according to plan**, because again, I not ever (told y'all I don't like that word) planned to join the military. The Army came to my house when I was a junior in high school. Not sure how they got my address or had a thought that I was interested because I wasn't. I was sick in bed with cramps and do you know my grandma made me get up and talk to this man??? Number one, I didn't want to go to the military. Number two, I would not even consider the Army if I had. Number three, I chose the Navy a year later, because number four, the Air Force didn't even look up at my face when I walked into their office. I can't stand the Air Force (joking).

CHAPTER THREE

I AM NOT A DEPENDENT

CHAPTER 3: I AM NOT A DEPENDENT

Raise your hand if you loathe that word, dependent 🙋. According to Lexical, there are three definitions. Let's discuss them. The first one is not important; it merely states "contingent upon or determined by." The second one states, "requiring someone or something for financial, emotional, or other support." The last one states, "unable to do without." Can we discuss these? Maybe because I was raised mainly by women from ages 12-19, I never understood or was taught how to be fully dependent on a spouse. My grandmother always worked, my mom here and there. My aunts, minus one, and female cousins all worked. So, to be dependent on someone for ALL of my needs and being called a dependent was foreign to me. Remember, I came from the military lifestyle, so I never liked being referred to as that. I bet men came up with that word for us ladies (just a thought). Saying the word dependent to grown adults almost seems condescending. I mean, my kids are dependent. They came in the world with that luxury, but calling me that, after coming from a career and working since I was sixteen, almost made me feel like I was back living with my grandma. I know some may read this and say it's a little extreme and not much of a big deal, but it is for me. The last definition, 'unable to do without,' just makes my blood boil. As a soldier, then spouse, I've seen enough marriages dissolve to know that I didn't want to be completely dependent on anybody. I have seen marriages fail in the military, where the spouse was so far away from family and solely reliant on their spouse for survival, that they had no way back home. I know you have seen them too. One of my greatest friends had this struggle when she divorced. I do want to add that her glow-up has been amazing! She is in real life, a beautiful butterfly. Now, I am not saying that I wanted to take care of me in case of divorce. I am saying that the word dependent feeds into your mind and makes you believe that a life of independence is not an option as a spouse. As a therapist, I believe the words we tell ourselves is what we believe to be. From early on, I knew I wanted more. I knew I would be more. As a new spouse, I hung on to that dream, even when I didn't believe it fully. There were times where my faith was so small, but it did not leave me. My friends and I plan to drop so many nuggets to you in this anthology. But if you don't take much away from this, I do want you to take this: **Change your language.** What you feed yourself is what you become. Feed yourself powerful words and you will be powerful. Feed yourself words of success and you will be a success. Tell yourself daily who your future self will be. You are powerful, you are successful, you are confident, and you are not a dependent. **You are your soldier's spouse.**

CHAPTER FOUR

THE MISTAKES I MADE

CHAPTER 4: THE MISTAKES I MADE

What they don't tell you about trying to do it all is, you crash. So, check this out, on my road to trying to be Miss Independent and all of the things, I crashed. Oh, and this happened twice, because obviously I didn't learn my lesson the first time. In Jan 2011, my husband was eight months into his deployment. Wait, let me back up a bit. Charlie, my husband, left in 2010 on our first deployment as a married couple. The deployment was ten months long, our daughter was two months old, and I was maybe three months removed from the military. Around the time he left, I believe my postpartum depression (which I didn't know I had until I became a therapist years later) had diminished. I had worked since I was able to work, so naturally, I went back to work. The process was long, but several months later, I worked as a DoD Police Officer for Keesler Air Force Base. I was so excited to be getting back to myself and back to work. I found Laila a daycare and they even took her early mornings. My first day of work, I was so exhausted. I realized that my 12-hour shift was really a 14-hour day. I worked 6 a.m.-6 p.m., and what that really looked like was 5 a.m.-7 p.m. This lasted for eight weeks. With all the training, clearances, and multiple interviews, I realized that I was driving myself into the ground AND another family was taking care of my child. Don't do that. You don't have to run yourself into the ground where you miss out on your family. There will be times where your schedule may cause you to be away for some time, but my schedule was ridiculous. A couple of months later, I went to Gulf Coast Community College and started working towards my associate's degree. My husband returned home two months later.

In 2011/2012-ish, I was in undergraduate. I was also working at Kay Jewelers, which I loved. I would also like to point out that I was offered part time work on the Gulfport Seabee Base. I believe it was between $14-$17 an hour. Y'all, I couldn't turn that down. So, here I was, less than a year later, trying to do all the things again. Apart of this was conditioning as a woman of color; a large part of it was. So, here I was, two jobs, full time school, and a toddler. My husband made a comment one day about me never seeing our kid. The one who was just on a ten month deployment, then headed out for an eight month deployment had the nerve to tell me that I wasn't present?? I was so hurt, partly because it was true, so I dropped the part time job with the quickness. Ten years later, I always think of that when I feel I am away in my office for too long. Family is important to me, and I try to ensure that each one of them feel the love from me in the way that they need. On your way to success, don't forget about those you come home to. They need you too.

CHAPTER FIVE

THE TRIED AND ~~FAILED~~ UNSUCCESSFUL GIGS

CHAPTER 5: THE TRIED AND ~~FAILED~~ UNSUCCESSFUL GIGS

As a milspouse, we love independent streams of income via multi-level marketing. It seems like it is a rite of passage for us, ha ha. We sell and when we look to purchase, we do so in our community. Many people believe these businesses are scams and some may be, I don't know. Some of them have been around for a long time and are proven to be a success. When my daughter was two, while I was in undergraduate and working at the bank, I got suckered into Mary Kay. As an introvert, I'd already felt it was not for me, but I did it anyway. I had major support in the beginning, but I was horrible at sales. When I stopped working at the base, I worked at Kay Jewelers briefly and even though I hit my sales goals monthly, I never did great with Add-Ons and Credit Card applications. The goal was to get at least one credit card app monthly and many months I did not hit that mark. The way I saw it was if someone really wanted a credit card or wanted to add earrings to their necklace purchase, then they would do it, so why did I have to try and force it? So yeah, sales was not my thing, but I had fun with Mary Kay. It took me out of my shell for a bit and then it was gone.

Scentsy was great. I was brought on by a milspouse a couple of years later and did it for three years when we were stationed in Wichita Falls. It was easy because people loved it so much that I did not have to sell it the way I did Mary Kay. Now, people loved Mary Kay also, but some felt they could go to the local store and get lipstick. Again, I will not convince you to do anything. With Scentsy, I did parties and local events, etc. It was different and the products were nothing that you had ever seen. I never held a lot of inventory because that could really bite you in the behind. I have seen that with so many spouses who'd sold other products and had gotten stuck with so much inventory, it was crazy. I only kept a bunch of bars that I knew I would use. Their parties were good and I even went to their conference. I absolutely loved it, until I didn't. Now, don't get me wrong,

Scentsy did nothing wrong and I didn't fall out of love with it, but moving so much, it just wasn't something that I could hang on to any longer. During this time, I was also in graduate school and had another business. Upon moving, losing my local connections was a bummer and I really did not want to do the work of rebuilding all over again, so I sold briefly when we went back to Mississippi and that was it.

During my time in Texas, I had a home daycare. Carlos, our second child, was born six months after we arrived and two months after I started graduate school. Can we pause so I can admit that I did not know what slow meant at this point? Upon moving, I told Charlie I had no plans to work and his response was, "Okay." That lasted six months. Laila went to school and Carlos was home with me, so I had an idea to open an in-home daycare so he could have support and we could make extra money. Again, I just did not know how to sit down. The daycare was such a great business and there were some days I'd overextended myself being up all day, then I'd be up all night for graduate school. Because I'd given everyone else everything and took care of myself when they all went to sleep, I was burning out. It was not fair that I was up until 1 a.m. and everyone else was having sweet dreams because Kasey Sacrifice King took time to ensure everyone's needs were met, so I made changes that turned all of that around and I could implement more me time. The daycare really wasn't unsuccessful, but I figured I'd throw it in here. When we moved, we found a building to make a legit business, but then a hurricane came through and wiped it out. Dream gone. Stargaze Childcare Center was the name I was going to give it. To stargaze is to observe the sky, stars, and everything beautiful out of space. There was no limit and that is what I wanted to teach my daycare kids. I want you to know this too. Whatever you do in life, only you can set that limit. If it is limitless, then your life will be beyond your wildest dreams, and you will continuously surprise yourself.

When I moved back to Mississippi, I met Tajh in a spouse group on Facebook. She wanted information on moving to Mississippi and the queen of living in the 'Sip was at her service. We had never met in person but talked every day. She was selling Pampered Chef at the time, and I purchased a cold brew pitcher from her. We bonded over coffee and I went to look at a house she was thinking of moving into. She seemed like someone I'd known forever. Her story is pretty amazing too. There is literally nothing she won't try; nothing. I love that about her, how personable and bold she is. Tajh started selling Scentsy under me for her own perks and a year later, started selling Lipsense. Now, Lipsense was this new and genius way to wear lipstick all day. There was a two-step process with an application at mid-day and then something to help you take it off in the evening. Why did I start selling that? I was back into makeup; you would think I would have learned better. Do you want to know how brief that was? End of story, not long at all.

The reason I almost stated that I'd failed at these things is because my success had not come. But how do you measure that? By the pink Cadillac? Some people have actually been successful, even when you look outside of measuring their success by their finances. I am still friends with Erin and have kept two of her kids. I love her so much and wish she and the kids were my next door neighbors. I met SheKendra during this time. That was seven years ago and we still talk almost every dang day. I have learned so much about business, which I use to this day. I learned a lot about forming relationships that my introverted self did not know before. I am grateful for these things (still could have done without Lipsense) and will always talk about how they have contributed to who I am today.

CHAPTER SIX

DIGGING MY WAY OUT OF DEPRESSION

CHAPTER 6: DIGGING MY WAY OUT OF DEPRESSION

In 2019, life was going great. I felt as if I'd finally found my footing. The kids were doing great in Mississippi and I was stepping into life a couple years after graduate school and loving my job. I felt like this was all that I'd worked so hard for and why I'd gone to school for seven plus years. I had gotten a job doing community mental health counseling. Now, let me tell you, this was not my favorite job, but I learned so much and it really prepared me to step into my dream role down the line. The thing I enjoyed about working with children and families in the home is I got to see them in their environment and their comfort zone. It helped them to ease into therapy with their guard down in a place that they controlled. I was completely okay with that because I am a believer in safe spaces and not always doing things the traditional way. After one year of driving from Gulfport to Picayune, Ocean Springs, Gautier (if you have been there, you know those drives can be long), I moved to another department within the agency, which is the Children's Advocacy Center. Mind you, I had also done this for quite a while in Baton Rouge where I interned. (Possible trigger warning) I worked with children who were sexually and physically abused victims of a violent crime (trafficking, etc.) I never wanted to work with kids and yet this was the most rewarding job I'd ever had. To hold space for children who had been through so much trauma, took a part of me I did not know existed. There were draining moments also, especially being a mom and hearing abuse stories.

My job was going great, my team was amazing, and I truly enjoyed going to work every day. As a spouse, you know how this goes; we came up for orders. I always dreaded this but this time was the worst ever because I was up for promotion, about to start being supervisor for a team and was close to finishing my license. My family was only two hours away, which was good as well. Well y'all, my husband made chief the year prior and there were no billets available for me to remain there and transfer to another unit, so we had to go to Virginia or California (Port Hueneme to be exact). Our whole career, both together and separately, we'd made it our mission to avoid Va. We are Navy all the way, but we aren't gung ho. We always remained the Southern people we'd grown up to be and the military did not change us, so a military town like the seven cities was not for us. However, since we were retiring after this next duty station, California was too far away, so Va. it was. Oh and let me not leave this part out; when we were set to leave, our baby was two months old. So, to be sure that I am clear, let's run this down:

- Eight week old newborn
- Upcoming job promotion
- Almost done with therapy hours for licensure
- Kids are settled and happy
- My family is right up the road
   -I'd made great connections in the community

I went to work hurt every day because I could not tell them I was leaving. You know how that goes, so no need explain 😉. If any of you whom I worked with at the CAC is reading this now, I love you and I am sorry. You are truly my favorite work crew, post Navy career. Life was really great. I had finally arrived and could let my shoulders down, or so I thought. We tried hard to stay. There were people who appeared to look out for Charlie but didn't, so we did the only thing we could do. As you know, there is only one choice when you get orders; leave. I have since learned that spouses stay in their careers while the solider goes to the next command. The only time I stayed behind was for a few months for graduation. I understand it now and I don't knock them for it. Thinking back, I still would not have stayed, yet I respect spouses who decide for themselves and their children not to bounce around. Have you ever considered staying behind? Or are you a mom that did? It's tough picking up your dreams and trying to rebuild somewhere else. Sometimes you just wanna throw all the reminders in the attic and say, "F-it, I will just watch tv and take the kids to school for the next three years."

When we left that summer for Va., I was depressed. Being a new mom again that pumped six to seven times a day, while taking care of two other children and working, I had all of the negative feelings. Let's count them down: I was angry, hurt, frustrated, but most of all depressed. When they speak of the sacrifices we make as spouses, they don't mention possible depression. Eleven years in and I had not seen it yet. I'd fought so hard to ensure that I did not lose myself and that I'd maintained whatever control over what I could, but this time was different. This time, there was no family to go to, much like when we were in Wichita Falls several years prior. There was no job waiting on me and here we were, sending our kids to a whole new school again. Now, don't get me wrong, we had family there, my husband's brother and sister. We even had to live with them very briefly when we first arrived, so that was something, until it wasn't, but I will get to that part shortly.

Two months after our arrival, my cousin passed away. Roughly two months later, my aunt passed away. Not being able to fly to those services with a new baby that I was nursing depressed me even more. By the time we had been there a full year, I had another death in the family; my grandmother. I lived with her until I left for the military, so I tell people my parent died. Three weeks before she passed, we went to visit her and I knew when I came back, it would be to bury her. I was out running early the morning of July 27, 2020 when my mom called and said, "Kasey, she's gone." I said, "kay," and hung up, then walked home crying. It felt like my chest was caving in. The woman who I credit for pretty much all of the great things that have happened in my life and who I always called to tell about all of my successes and challenges, left this world. The woman who would still send cards and checks for birthdays and anniversaries, was no longer. In that moment, I went blank. So let's check in: twelve months in Virginia, lost my starting career, lost my cousin, aunt, and grandma. Oh wait, six months after moving, COVID hit. By the way, my kids caught COVID five months after our arrival and two months before they figured out what it was. COVID affected a lot of things. Earlier, I mentioned Charlie's brother and sister; they were great until COVID. We saw them often and Priscilla was so great to us. She would come and see the kids and a couple of times, Charlie and I were able to have date nights. Her presence always lit the house up and the kids loved her so much. Things ended around March 2020 because COVID closed everyone's doors. Being in the dark sucks and it can be a hard place to crawl out of. Some days, I was really mad at Charlie for not retiring. He always said, "Anything after twenty belongs to you." Then, it was like, "Oh wait, I need to do three more years to get this High Three." I understood, but I did not care. My family was leaving this world and I could not be present. I was living, but not existing. This was truly a time when moms "put on the brave face" so your kids would not see you cry. All I did was cry in the beginning. I am sure I cried from mid-2019 to mid-2021. I was a ball of a mess. Don't get me wrong, great things happened during that time too, but I was pushing through while in grief mode. I am always a **glass half full** person and I knew better was coming, so I tried my best to focus on the light to dig my way out. When you do this, you will you gain so much clarity and a new, beautiful sense of self.

LET'S TALK ABOUT THESE TEARS

Two months before my grandmother passed, I started therapy. I knew that I needed to get a handle on things and to prepare myself for grief; but too late. I was already dealing with so much that I probably should have started right after the move, or even the first death, but it came at the time it was needed most, I guess. My therapist was great and I wish I could have brought her with me when I moved. What I would like to mention during this time, was two things that happened; well three. For a few years at this point, I had been trying to past my licensing exam. I'd taken it so many times, I just knew at this point that I was dumb and I'd gone as far as getting a psychological test done to determine my intelligence. Of course, I was told that my IQ was normal and there was nothing that would prevent me from passing; just maybe General Anxiety Disorder. At this point, I had taken this test six times across three states (Louisiana, Alabama and Virginia). Mississippi did not even have a testing center, so I always drove an hour to test. Now in Va., I had taken it and failed again, not realizing that I'd only been in the city for maybe a month, with a newborn and was depressed as all get out. I wasn't listening to my body. Maybe I hadn't learned the valuable lesson in community because outside of briefly studying with Jess and another group of ladies prior, I never leaned on anyone. It wasn't until I finally met a group of ladies that helped me see it all through. In this community that we are in, not having support is hard. We do everything ourselves and most of the time, we have ourselves to blame. As adults, we like to follow this "no new friends" trend and it does us no bit of good. Many of the tears I shed, I shed them alone. There were a few people on my last two or three test tries that held space for me because I was finally starting to get it. Charlie was a great support too. The reason I kept going was because I had to prove to myself that I could do it and I wanted to teach my kids not to give up. Reader, wherever you are right now in your journey, don't give up. There are people who need what you have to offer, so don't allow anything to bring up so much fear in you that you say "F-it."

One day, my baby was crying and I remember sitting on the end of the bed holding him and crying too. Failing tests, death, new baby and all, I was thinking, "God, what now?" This was months before I'd started a job and I literally did not know what was next. Sometimes, that's a great thing because it forces you to sit with yourself and discover the greatest parts of you. I knew I would not be a therapist in Virginia. I knew that I was not going through that process again, but I had all the skills to guide people, couples specifically. A new dream manifested in me to reach as many couples as possible through coaching.

This was funny and I laughed when the message was given to me. As a therapist, we don't like coaches. This was when I really did not know anything about coaches because I stayed in my lane. I will always be a therapist, so I knew I would pick that back up after Virginia, but for now, coaching was my new focus. It stretched me to many unknown territories and put me in places unimaginable. I still mourned my losses, Sylvia Faye, Teedee, and Maw Maw; however, I no longer mourned the loss of my job because in that darkness, I'd found a new way to achieve a greater dream. It is possible that your dream may be deferred and you may have to shelve some ideas. Your kids may be home for the summer and your spouse may be deployed. Or maybe the stars just aren't aligning right now—and that is okay. You may not be able to go back to school for your teaching certification right now, but you may be able to tutor. Maybe you can create a series of videos on topics that you taught your kids and sell them. There is always more than one way to skin a cat, so for that, I stopped crying about leaving my job and started honing in on this newly found venture. Again, there is and place for everything. If it is not your time right now, that is okay. It will come, therefore, keep that journal of ideas and one day it will come to fruition.

In the midst of launching my coaching business, I started a new job a month later. I knew it was temporary, but I had my reasons. For starters, I wanted an escape. I was home with three kids many days and left to my thoughts, so when my oldest two started school, I needed an escape. Also, I knew we would be buying a house the following year and I thought it would be wise to save. Lastly, I would be out of job again at some point, so I wanted to prepare myself by saving, and also funneling my business. So, this job was not only for my self-care, but it would make life less hard in the future.

The reason this falls into the tears category is because while launching my business and working a full time job, I was still studying for this dang on exam! I opened myself up, found a large group, and studied five days a week, for two hours, from 8 p.m.-10 p.m. Sometimes, while trying to wait up for me, Charlie would listen to me study, but would fall asleep at the voice of Raquel. One month after I started my job and COVID hit, I had to take my job home AND homeschool. Again, when I'd finally found an escape, I ended up being right back at the house. But whatever, we are spouses and we always make it happen, right? So, I worked from home from 1 p.m.-9 p.m. and jumped in the study group during the last hour of my shift. Throughout everything that I did and went through, the exam was always on my priority list. I was so dedicated that I would push the phone under the bed and stuff a pillow on top when a work call came through. "Thank you for calling Military OneSource. This call is recorded for quality assurance. Is that okay?" or something like that. I took care of business, then went back on the Zoom. Groups were Monday through Friday, some Saturdays for us dedicated folks, and briefly on Sunday for me. The first time I took the exam with that group, I failed by five points. At this time, I'd failed so much, it was whatever, but I never stopped studying, so I was right back in it. January 2021, four years after graduating, eight tests later, and helping other folks pass on their first try, it was finally my turn. I PASSED!!! The tears of emotional exhaustion turned into tears of joy. The crazy thing is, the last time I walked into that testing center, I knew I would pass. Like, I really knew and there was no doubt. I was in the car right before in a therapy session and walked out knowing that victory was mine. Victory is yours too. You just have to see it. When things don't go our way during the moment that we prefer, we give up. Had I passed four years ago, I would have been able to help all of the people that I tutored to pass. Yes, it hurt to help them pass when I couldn't, but maybe, just maybe, I was the vessel for their success so that I could learn that success is not always what I do for me, but the service that I give to others. Milspouse, we service our spouses in ways that other spouses don't. I'm not saying that our sacrifice is greater, but it's different. We sacrifice as a service to the country we swore (as spouses) to support. You are a success, no matter where you are in life. You just have to believe it too!

THE ROAD TO DISCOVERING YOU

I teach spouses all the time not to lose themselves (military or not). You may have seen a message on my IG, TikTok or Facebook if you follow me. Through coaching and therapy, I see many women (some men too) that get so lost in the life of being a parent, spouse, employee, etc. that they forget about themselves. What happens when you forget about you? I can tell you what I have felt and/or been told. Nod (even though I won't see it) if you've felt any of these:

- Lonely
- Angry
- Resentful
- Emotionally exhausted
- Physically tired all the time

When you are disconnected from you, you feel as if you are on autopilot. You move throughout the day, but it is to service others, much like a robot. That brings no joy to you. Our first time in Mississippi, I worked all those jobs at once, thinking it was servicing my family. I did what I thought was right, but also in fear. Here I was pouring heavy into this role that is not mine and doing what I was taught (or saw) my grandmother do. She robot-ed her way through life. She was a provider for everyone except herself. Almost two years had passed since I separated from the military and I was still in soldier mode. I had to slow down. I took time for sure, but on that path to discovering me, I put me first.

Many women are taught to serve and men to provide, so we are all worker bees, in some sort, in a role that sometimes does us no good internally. As a military spouse, it is so easy to lose yourself, especially when many times you are trying to fill the role of both parents. I can tell you this, though, when you discover who you are, it will all come together. You are more than a spouse, I am pretty sure you already know that, but are you living it? Are you living a life for you that still pours into your family? Are you working weekly towards your personal goals? Outside of your spouse and kids, what is for you? Not what is left for you, but what is for you? On the next few lines, I want you to answer these questions:

1. I am:

_____

_____

2. I love to:

_____

_____

3. My desire in life is to:

_____

_____

4. Internal peace to me looks like:

_____

_____

5. I take care of myself daily by:

_____

_____

When you discover you, you learn how powerful you are. You discover that you are peace for many people. You may also discover that some things you were taught were completely wrong or were not taught at all. I have talked to many people who thought they knew love until they were loved correctly. I've talked to people who were millionaires and not at peace. So this is not about money or external relationships, it is about your relationship with you. I even had to learn this when working those jobs. What was I really after? Was it peace? Or independence? Was I trying to follow my dreams? Or not be so dependent on my husband, much like my grandma? I had to really sit and be with myself to figure out why my direction was so important and who it was serving.

On your journey to finding you, you can BS a lot of people, but **not yourself**. Your shadow is the one thing that never leaves you while you are walking this earth. The shadow connected to me was filled with habits resulting from being raised by a woman running herself in the ground. Also, a woman that loved so hard, that her running in the ground had purpose. I was running myself into the ground ten years ago, because I felt it was beneficial for everyone else, but I never asked my husband his thoughts. I remember in 2016, I mentioned to my husband that I was tired of doing "all the things." Do you know what this man said to me? He said, "That's your fault. No one told you to do that." Even when we feel we are giving our best, and doing the most, how do we know whether it's expected or if it's learned behavior?

Had I talked to my husband early on and asked the right questions, I probably would've finished this book four years ago. At the same time, four years ago, it would have been just me and not Tajh, Leah and SheKendra. So, in the midst of discovering me, I learned that the introverted me could not do it alone. I have learned so much about the importance of community. There are some things that I've gotten wrong on the road often traveled, but when I decided to change my course (internally) to the road less traveled, I found peace, clarity, support and am no longer stuck. I found me and I continuously welcome any new pieces I pick up along the way because we all are ever changing. Have you found you? What you will find is that the discovery never stops, it grows. I grew up surrounded by plants, thanks to my grandmother. She always had plants on the porch and it is one of my greatest memories of the houses we lived in. When you learn their needs and treat them right, they never stop growing. Sometimes, you must trim them, but they will continue to grow with love, water, and sun. Continue to give yourself love and trim the parts that no longer serve you. Give yourself water and sun; you will forever grow.

CREATING YOUR OWN IS A MISCONCEPTION

When I started the journey on this book several years and two states ago, I was driving to see a family in Picayune. Maybe I was salty about the sacrifices I had made as a spouse, or maybe I was proud of how far I had come and wanted to let other spouses know to never give up. Whatever success that comes to me is family success. What I mean by creating your own is not about separate living, secret accounts, or building something selfishly. You are talented and along the way, you left (or discovered) that talent and decided to shelve it for now (or maybe permanently). Creating yours is about not forgetting about you. It is about not having to continuously defer your life because you aren't sure how to make yourself a priority. It is about following the goals you have set for yourself and not having to wait twenty years (if you don't want).

On the road to creating your own lane, you are still your partner's spouse and your children's parent, so do not confuse "your own" for "your own life." I am sure you have worked hard to maintain the life you currently have. Marriage takes daily work and parenting is the most consistent thing you will ever do. Do not forget about them in the midst of creating your dreams. Outside of my bio in this book, I have not talked a lot about what I do. I am a Licensed Marriage and Family Therapist and I worked with couples daily on curating the marriage they desire. It takes time, even years for some, to swap the I's for Us. As you are creating or living in your purpose, do not allow it to ever come before your family. I was watching a video podcast on YouTube, I can't remember the name, but the man created this amazing platform and gained much success but stated he can't remember the last time he spent ten minutes with his wife. The marriage therapist in me was shocked, temporarily. Then I realized that quality time is often taken for granted and does not take precedence over work, oftentimes. When orders come up, your spouse lets you know and you decide which places work for the family, correct? Schools, neighborhood, surrounding areas, distance from family, jobs and all of the necessities. On this journey, don't forget to regard you partner in that same way. You are always a team.

COFFEE BEFORE WINE: LIFE OF A BUSINESS OWNER

As a business owner, you will hold several positions until you can afford to hire someone. Let's count them:

1. Admin
2. Accountant
3. Social Media Manager
4. Designer
5. CEO

Did I miss any? Let's not forget spouse and parent. We can break the duties down in those roles as well, but I want to save paper. Before this book, my other products were created 85-90% by me. With my first workbook, I had maybe six versions before I could release it. Every time I read it, I found an error. The cover art on my initial workbook came from Canva. I was the only one marketing it (yikes) and I had to ensure that it sold. My cards took over a year because I wrote them out myself, visioned the design in my head, found someone on Fiverr to do the design, uploaded them to a card site and BOOM. Doing everything alone takes a lot out of you. It takes the coffee kind of energy. Even if you don't drink coffee, to take on five positions in your business takes coffee energy, even during times where wine is the preference. I was in business for almost two years before I had a virtual assistant; it lasted for only four months. Not a knock against her, but it was just that I wasn't ready because I could really create the time and save money. Wine time decreased for me because I knew my goal required coffee. It required the full and present me. It required me to work when I did not want to work. Even writing this book has stretched me, not dreadfully, but it has challenged me. I did not always have the motivation to write. I did not always have the motivation to go live, create posts, or even create a darn content calendar. I still don't like content calendars, but they are a proven method that works. I had to ask myself what the end goal was to push me through at times. Look at it from a parenting perspective. Some days you want to stay in bed and say forget those kids, right? Let them fix their own cereal. You aren't motivated to fix breakfast, lunch, and take them to school every day, but you know it's necessary. Some of you are not looking to start a business. You may be looking to start school, get back on the job market, finish those certifications, or lose weight. You don't always need motivation; you need discipline. As I am writing this, I ate dinner late with the family and immediately stepped away. Without discipline, many things in my life would not be accomplished. Wine energy is okay when you need moments to relax, recenter yourself, and spend time with your spouse. I will always say don't lose sight of that, but at the same time, don't lose sight of your goal. All those things can be done without overextending yourself. When I create a list of my goals, or think of what may be next for me, I may get wine energy (not gonna lie). I think "whooo, that is a lot. I'm good." Then, I immediately tell myself that God would not have planted this in me if someone didn't need it. There are people that are waiting on you. If you are selling makeup, crafting, tutoring, teaching, or nursing, there are people every day that need what you have to offer. So, everyday coffee energy is a must. And let me clarify; this does not mean eight hours daily. Creating an outline, scheduling, meal planning, etc., could take as little as an hour daily. The world is waiting on you, my spouse in arms. Are you going to answer?

THE TOOLS TO SUCCESS

As a spouse, parent and entrepreneur, I have one thing fighting against me; time. Don't you hate when people say, "we all have the same 24 hours?" Whatever. I literally cannot stand that statement, no matter how true it is. When people tell me they don't have time, I used to say, "but you do" and point out time in their schedule where things could be done. I still believe this, but our lives are so different, so I do not judge. Instead, I try to meet them where they are. It can be hard, but I have come to understand that we are all different and the same 24 hours may be different to a mom of four with a spouse on a one year deployment than one with no kids and a spouse on a one year deployment. I have written this book all over my house (bedroom, kitchen table, couch, guest bedroom, family room, and office) during all different times of the day. I've written for twenty minutes, two hours, one hour, etc. I found time to make this happen, even when I felt there was no time.

My last coach, Jai, made over $200K last year as a single mom living in her mom's basement. She discussed her divorce, moving home with her preteen, and putting a plan in motion. There is another mom who rose to fame over the past year also. She has four kids, recently left an abusive marriage, and moved home with her mom. She used her stimulus check to start a business and made one million a year later. So, maybe we all have the same time, but again, I do not judge. I do know that the similarity between the two of them is determination. They came from divorces with nothing or little to nothing and vowed not to go backwards. There are many others. We also have many milspouse moms who are successfully doing their thing. Again, success is not about the money you generate, but the manner in which you are attaining your goals. To these ladies, their goals are freedom, independence, and something to pass down to their children. My goals are to save marriages, display love and a positive marriage to my kids, financial freedom, and a life where my kids can have better opportunities than me. I didn't have money for school, I was not pushed to go to college or even helped with completing an application. I was not given the support that I needed. I was not equipped for life when I left the house. I learned on my own.

My success is determined by how my family sees me. Do they see that I am being as successful in parenting as other areas in my life? Being successful as a wife and mom is always my priority. Being a success in business is always a goal, but not my number one goal. I will tell you what my process looks like to create success in more than one area of my life.

> 1. Communication. I always communicate my expectations to my spouse whenever a transition comes about. Whether this is a new military move, job, business opportunity, etc. I discuss with him what my life will look like professionally and if that works for him. I then discuss with my kids the schedule outside of the home for me, so they can have an open book to my life. I always touch bases with them and check in about my parenting. I tell them my schedule and when I may get really busy and need alone time. Some don't do this or believe in this. My mom and grandparents never did this. I like to know how I am doing and if I am not giving attention in areas that are needed. As parents and spouses, we need to slow down and tune in also.
>
> 2. Boundaries. I am a firm believer in boundaries. I no longer have a problem saying no. I am no longer the people pleaser I grew up to be. I will tell my husband no...and his kids (ha ha). With them, I give an explanation though, so don't think I just say no and walk off. Some things are not always

feasible; that's the truth. Some things just can't be done just because they want it done. I try to set a clear line so I can take care of the necessary things in my business, and sometimes that means a trip to Five Below will be deferred.

3. I don't balance my life. For the record y'all, there is no such thing. None of my obligations will get equal time. I don't look at equality, but priority. Whatever is in front of me at that moment is my priority. Super early mornings are reserved for me (and sometimes my husband). Early mornings (8:30 a.m. during the summer) are reserved for family, mid-mornings to early evenings are reserved for work, late evenings are for family, and nighttime is for my husband. You will run yourself into the ground trying to ensure everyone has equal access to you. Instead, ensure the time you give to every part of your life feels it. You want your spouse to feel the love when you are together and your kids. You want time to connect with yourself first and feel ready to take on anything. Then, you want the other things that you are directing your energy towards to feel it. That is how you measure quality. Balance is necessary.

4. Find your tribe. Many people are okay with their spouse and kids. I am not sure I could be because some things are reserved for friends. Not everything needs to cross the threshold of your spouse. This does not mean keep secrets, this means there are some things I need my friends, coach, or therapist for. I should have taken advantage of the spouse community earlier. The introverted me would not allow myself to until halfway into our marriage. I found out where people are that have interests like me. In Virginia, I joined a milspouse soccer team and had the time of my life. The

deployment prior, I tried my best to attend all FRG meetings (in Gulfport). Milspouse or not, find your support system, cheerleaders, business besties and goal friends.

Business success is important because it determines whether it lasts or not. Whether you are a baker, business coach, tutor, or crafter it must generate something consistently for it to be considered a successful business. So, you must invest time into it. No matter what field you are in this applies. And again, don't forget about your network. Find spouses who are like-minded. Not all are messy, as they say. Find some that understand you and understand that you won't always be able to go out, but are always supportive in your journey and vice versa. When I let go, I found this and it has helped me become better in so many ways.

When I finally allowed myself to let go, I met Tajh who inspired me so much with all her talents and fearlessness. Leah is like the godmom of milspouses. She has been in this for so long and inspires others on so many levels. I love the way she loves her family and keeps them at the center. SheKendra never gives up and is one of the best moms I know. There were times I would wonder how she does all the things she does. She is superwoman for real. I hope their stories inspire you to never give up on you. That you are more than a spouse and mom. You are everything you desire to be, even if that is a spouse and mom. I get hot when moms tell me, "I'm just a stay-at-home parent." Excuse me? "Just?" Don't do that. That requires so much of you. Don't even diminish that. It takes a lot of you to pour into your family daily, so don't ever think you should be doing more if that is not your desire. I have said it before and I will say it again, success is relative and is not about finances. It is about how you define it. If your goal is to do more and create more, then do more and create more. If your goal is to be the best parent and spouse, then be the best and celebrate each step. In fact, I want to celebrate you now and say thank you. Thank you for doing a very hard job daily. Thank you for taking on the task of marrying someone you may barely see, making the sacrifices you make daily, supporting other spouses from pure kindness, and being you. Thank you.

It is my hope that you take whatever you need from this book and the stories of my friends. I get you, I am you, I see you, and I will always hold space for you. We are this secret village that will go to bat for each other without ever meeting or speaking lol. We will discuss which branch is better, but have each other's backs regardless. I look forward to Army/Navy games each year and am still salty about the Air Force rejecting me, but let someone outside of our bubble have an issue with us, no matter what branch, and I will still have your back. I am so proud to be a spouse of someone who was willing to lay his life on the line for me every single day. It does not get better than that. Thank your spouse for me too.

ACKNOWLEDGMENTS

Juanita: My dearest grandmother who I miss every day. Lavender Healing Center, my therapy practice was named after her. Her favorite color is purple and birthstone amethyst. I do everything hoping she'd approve. I hope even though you are no longer physically present, I am making you proud.

Jamie Miller Brown: You have done so much for me the past several years. I could not have gotten through many moments without you. I thank you for checking on me during deployments, listening to my cries over this exam and actually being able to understand because we both are spouses and in the same field. I never felt like I was whining when talking you; just releasing. Thank you for always holding space for me. Truly the best mentor ever!

Charlie: Thank you for never asking me to change. You continuously accept me as I am and support my craziest ideas. You have always been the most supportive husband and I am so thankful to have you in my life.

Laila, Carlos, and Bernard: You bring such a joy to my life, even on the days you work my nerves. I always just watch in awe of how Daddy and I have created the best kids. Having you three has really stretched me to find new and creative ways to work, to be more patient, and to know what true love is. Thank you for your patience, understanding, and thank you boys for always thanking me for my service every night. I love you.

LEAH HUGGINS

CHAPTER SEVEN

A BAG OF
HER OWN

CHAPTER 7: A BAG OF HER OWN

The truth is, I was my own person before I met my husband. I had my own dreams, my own plans, and my own goals. As far back as I can remember, I always knew that I was destined for greatness. I just didn't know how or what that greatness would look like.

I come from a two-parent home. Both were working. My dad was a fire chief, and my mom was an executive secretary. Although my dad was the breadwinner, it took both of their incomes to run the house.

My mom always worked. Sometimes, she would bring me to her office, and I would watch her in action. She'd give me a piece of paper to write or to color on and I would sit there and watch her answer phones or work from her desk. She would have conversations with her co-workers, using big, important words that I didn't understand. My dad gave me an old phone and a manual typewriter to play with, and I would pretend that I was answering calls and running the office just like my mom. She was my example. I grew up with the understanding that I was supposed to work.

I went through a lot of career choices as a kid. Of course, the first thing I wanted to be was a superhero, like Wonder Woman. But that dream was short lived, mostly because I couldn't fly (no matter how hard I tried), and because my mom was not going to let me walk around in my underwear to fight crime. I was really into gymnastics, and the moment I learned how to do a round-off, I knew I was destined for Olympic greatness, but I soon realized that my dedication to the sport would take away all the fun time I wanted to have playing outside with my friends. In high school, I spent some time with a child psychologist and thought that would be a great field for me to work in, but my grades said otherwise.

I went to college and had a ball! I lived the college experience to the fullest. In fact, I had so much fun that I forgot to go to all my classes and ended up back home in my parents' house. That's when it happened. My mom gave me an ultimatum. She told me that two grown women can't live in the same house, and she gave me a week to join the military. She didn't even care which branch, I just had to get on the next thing smoking. This is how I ended up in the Navy.

I worked in construction, which is a field dominated by men. Day after day, I listened to them tell stories and complain about their wives. It was from those conversations that I began to form an image in my mind of what a typical military wife was like. In short, her life was centered around serving her husband. Since she was not the one that made the money, she had little say over what went on in her house. Because he was the breadwinner, he called all the shots. He was the one in control and she was dependent on her husband to take care of her.

By the time I met my husband, I was on my way out of the military. I was a single mom and had planned to finish my time and get out so I could go back home with my baby. We had come from two different places and had two totally different opinions of how to manage and spend money. He was a saver, and I was a spender, so, as you can imagine, we had some pretty intense conversations over the years about our finances. And dare I say, it almost broke us up a few times.

We struggled financially for a long time, especially after I got out of the military. I tried being a stay-at-home mom, but I soon learned that was not my calling. Don't get me wrong, I am a great mom, nobody can take that from me, but everyone is not equipped to be a homemaker full time, and there is no shame in that. Being a stay-at-home mom is not an easy thing to do. If it was easy, then anyone could do it. You are graced to do what you are called to do. That means you are able to do with ease what others struggle to do.

So, I decided to go back to school, not because I had finally chosen an amazing career path, but because the VA benefits brought in a nice amount of money, which my family needed. I worked as a receptionist in my kids' daycare to reduce the cost for them to attend. I even started a catering service, which was pretty successful for a few years.

Looking back, I realize that I was just floating through life, not making things happen, just being and letting the chips fall where they might. I was in survival mode. Finances were not the only problem I was facing in my marriage. After two tours to Iraq during wartime, my husband was diagnosed with PTSD, among other things. While PTSD does come with its own set of problems, it is not the cause of all the problems in a marriage. In fact, what PTSD does is to highlight the problems that already exist in that marriage.

Times were rough and the environment of our home became toxic. There were times that I feared for my safety, and for his as well. At one point, I wanted to leave, but I could not afford it. Can you imagine? Having to stay in a toxic relationship because you simply cannot afford to leave? I felt like a failure. I had failed at marriage, I failed my kids, and I had failed at life. If anything, a mother should be able to take care of her kids. It's a terrible position to be in where the one person you were dependent on to live was no longer around. I felt helpless.

In my past, I have experienced financial abuse. Because I was not the breadwinner, the one paying for everything used money to control me. If I didn't do what that person wanted me to do, then I would be cut off financially and not able to survive. This is a fear-based control tactic to keep you dependent on the abuser. So, I had to go along with the person paying the bills. During an argument, I've had keys to the car I drive taken from me. I've been threatened to be kicked out of my own house, yes, the one with my name on it. Needless to say, I developed trust issues and got to the point where I refused to have anything else that someone could take away from me. I made up in my mind that I would make my own money and pay my own bills. The question was HOW would I do this?

I was at a pretty low point in my life. Fear, anxiety, doubt, and depression were all controlling me. I knew I needed a change. Something on the inside longed for more.

Around the same time that all of this was going on, my husband was preparing for a six-month deployment. I knew that I had to use this time out to get myself together. That is my first tip for you. Take advantage of the time you have to yourself. As a mom and wife, we are constantly pulled in all directions, catering to everyone but ourselves. Eventually, that can be overwhelming. It is in times like these that a reset is just what is needed to get us back on track. I used the time apart created by my husband's deployment for self-care and personal development. That deployment changed my life.

To begin with, I committed to a relationship with God. Now, I'm not talking religion, but real relationship. My spirit was dying, and I needed a fresh wind to resuscitate me. This set the foundation moving forward. The more I learned, the more I grew, and the stronger I became. My mindset was key. I had to break the patterns of negative thinking that had been controlling my life. I had to change the way I thought about things, in order to change the way that I looked at my situation. I had to change old habits like negative thinking which led to toxic behaviors. It took a lot of time, prayer, and hard work to do this.

Real change for me began with discovering my identity. I went on a journey of self-discovery to find out who I really am. It wasn't easy, and it wasn't always pretty. I learned that wife, mother, daughter, and friend are just titles. They do not define all of who I am. It is so important to discover and maintain your identity. As women, we are the anchor of the family. We set the tone in the home. Don't lose yourself in just being a spouse; forgetting the dreams and the plans you have for yourself. There is nothing wrong with being a mom or a wife. You are raising the future. As a spouse, your home is your first ministry. Ministry has to do with service. By serving your family, you build them in love and send them out into the world as healthy, whole, productive citizens that will help to make the world a better place.

Once I knew who I was, it was time to focus on the reason I am here. My purpose. We were created for connection. Purpose is always connected to someone else's need. The driving force of purpose is service.

Everyone born on the face of the earth has a purpose. You were born on purpose for a purpose. Whether it is to be a mom and wife, a CEO in the corporate world, or an entrepreneur, you are paving the way for your family. Being unfulfilled in life can lead to depression, low self-esteem, and it can stop you from achieving your goals.

It is your purpose that gives you your "WHY." Your "WHY" is your motivation. It is the thing that drives you and keeps you from quitting when you want to give up. The things that bother you the most, those issues that are so near and dear to your heart, those problems you would solve if you only had the resources to do so, those are all the things that point you toward your purpose. The things that pain you the most are the problems you are called to solve.

You are equipped for your purpose. You already have everything you need. Experience has been your teacher. What you have survived has become a lesson. You have learned from it, and you have grown from it. The pain of your past has a purpose, which is to develop you and to make you stronger. Now that you are out, you can share with the world how you were able to get out. Remember, someone is struggling with the very thing you have already made it through. You are proof that it can be done.

For me, purpose came wrapped up in my pain. The moment I took control of my life, everything changed, including my relationship with my husband… because I changed my focus. In 20 years, we've come a long way and grown, mainly by holding on to, growing in, and learning from my faith. By the grace of God, we gathered some tools along the way that we use to this very day.

I now encourage, support, and inspire other PTSD wives on their journey. My purpose has become my passion and now I have created a business around it.

While on my spiritual journey, I developed a set of principles that I know to be true. If you find your purpose, the money will find you. You don't have to chase paper! Make sure that you are pursuing the right thing. I struggled financially because I spent so much time trying to get money in ways that did not feed my soul. That's why it would never work out and I'd always have to find something different. I had to find my lane. No, I had to create my lane. Once I did that, financial opportunity opened up for me.

I had to learn to prioritize. First things first. As a military spouse, you are called to be wife, mother, or husband, father first. Your job is to support, making sure that the home is running efficiently. It is the home environment that determines productivity and morale in the workplace. When the home is right, it takes the pressure off the service member. They don't have to go to work stressed about what's going on in their home and their family life. They can focus their attention on their job and perform their duties better. And, yes, you can do this while working a 9 to 5 or while pursuing your entrepreneurial goals.

It's all about balance. Remember, you can do it all, you just can't do it all at the same time. Put systems in place to help you to avoid burnout. Adding a business to an already hectic schedule can be a disaster. Soon, you will be overwhelmed from being overworked. Learn how to budget your time and your energy.

Evaluate for dead weight. Those are the people, places, and things that are holding you back. They drain your energy and produce no good fruit in your life. I like to call them energy vampires. They will continue to suck the life out of you until you cut them off and put a stop to it. Who you surround yourself with can make or break you. Get around people that make you excited about the possibility of your future. Seek mentorship. Find the person that is successfully doing what you want to do and watch them. If you can, connect with them and see how you can serve them. This is the best way to gain experience in your field.

Your inner dialog matters. What you say to yourself can make or break you. Take it easy on yourself. Don't put too much pressure on yourself to perform. Make up in your mind that you are going to keep going with or without support. The truth is, sometimes you will have to do it by yourself. In marriage, you may find that support comes with limits. Sometimes, it seemed like my husband could not see my vision, which made it hard for him to support me. He would help me sometimes with my catering business, and we would end up fighting by the end of the night. We learned to stay in our lanes and decided that it would be better for me to work alone on some things. Of course, he would be there if I needed him to. But for the sake of our marriage, we had to come to an understanding of what his support would look like from a distance.

Be sure to pace yourself. Don't take on too much at one time. This can lead to stress and burnout. Start with a firm foundation and build from there. Learn as much as you can before launching out. Read. Read. Read. Study and sharpen your skills. Listen to podcasts and take some classes. You can even volunteer to work in your field to gain more experience. Don't be in a rush. Become valuable in your field. Establishing the right foundation first will save you time, money, and energy.

You have to be disciplined. Distractions will come to throw you off course. You will feel discouraged and want to give up, but you must hang in there. Consider this; what would happen if you stopped? If you give up, everything that is connected to you will die, too. All their dreams, plans, and goals will go right down the drain. You are the pattern. You are the solution. The world needs you to be who you were called to be.

I went from being a damsel in distress to being a warrior, champion, and provider for my family. I transformed my life, repurposed my pain, and reclaimed my power.

Every woman should have a bag of her own. She who holds the bag, holds the power to take control over her own life, make her own decisions, and be the master of her own destiny.

Be Encouraged. Be Empowered. Be Blessed.

SHEKENDRA COLLINS

CHAPTER EIGHT

MY NAME IS SHEKENDRA COLLINS

CHAPTER 8: MY NAME IS SHEKENDRA COLLINS

My Name is SheKendra Collins, formerly SheKendra Bailey. Because my mom, Kathleen, attended Alabama A & M University, I was born in Huntsville, AL. I was raised by a single parent in Linden, AL. Linden is a small town in West Alabama, about 15 miles from Demopolis, AL. If you blink your eyes, you will miss it. There are two stoplights. We lived most of our lives with my grandmother, Earlean, who was strict. She was the type of grandmother where your friends' parents had to call to ask if you could do anything and she still might say no. I know if it were not for my cousin Harley's mom, Ms. Denise Thomas, there would have been a lot of things I would have missed. If you called after 10, I could not talk on the phone. My best friend, Cynthia Lewis, knows this so well, along with any boys that dared to call. I had to be in the house when the streetlight came on. My cousin and I would play outside most of the time. I had to wash dishes, wash and hang clothes on the line, take the trash out, and keep my room clean. I am most grateful for these life skills learned early in life. The few times my mom and I did have a place of our own we lived in the projects.

While in elementary school, I would get up and my mom would make me oatmeal with milk and sugar. I would watch Gem and G.I. Joe before walking to school. Walking to school alone back then seems safer than it would be now. Times have certainly changed. I rode the bus to school when I was at my grandmother's. I was the first one on in the morning with Ms. Williams and the last one off in the evening. I did not really enjoy riding the bus because I was bullied sometimes, but my grandmother never owned a driver's license. I came home and did homework if I had not already done it at school. Since my grandmother did not have cable, I watched shows on ABC and CBS. There are popular shows to this day like Martin, Good Times, and 227 that I have not seen simply because we did not have cable. I watched a lot of college basketball, Wheel of Fortune, Jeopardy, soap operas, and sitcoms that came on in the evening.

I soon figured out to get out of the house I needed to involve myself in extracurricular activities at school, so in junior high, I joined the basketball team. I was never really any good at it, so by the time I got to high school I decided to try out for the cheerleading squad. This was my home. This was what I was good at. I was able to go to all the football and basketball games because I was a cheerleader, and as a member of the cheerleading squad you are also the dance team. This really helped get me out of the house and enhance my social life. While my classmates were playing around in class with our free time, I would be working on my homework so that when school was out and it was time for practice, I would have nothing to do once I got home. I wanted to keep my grades up because there was a GPA requirement for being a cheerleader, and I also liked helping my classmates with their homework when they had questions. So, it was a clever idea to have it done already. I always seemed to be a multitasker, having a full plate year-round. After high school, I went to Tuskegee University to study mathematics. I pledged Zeta Phi Beta Sorority, Inc., and served as vice president, president, and step mistress. After graduation, I was accepted into graduate school at Auburn University where I studied applied mathematics and math education while I was a graduate teaching assistant. I taught math classes on campus, tutored, and had office hours in addition to my studies.

When I graduated from Auburn, I accepted a job as a group manager at Anheuser-Busch, Inc., in Cartersville, GA. This was my first taste of corporate America in a production-based setting, and I did not like it at all! In January, midway through my first year, I had to have surgery to have my gallbladder removed. I'd gone to the doctor for a consultation since I kept getting sick after

I ate at work. Since there was a six-week recovery, my mom and my boyfriend, Jammieon Collins, came down to help me after the surgery. The surgery was a success. Jamie stayed for two weeks before returning to Rapid City, SD, where he was stationed at Ellsworth AFB. My mom stayed the entire time. I was blessed to have her there to help me. When I went back to work, I felt much better. By February, I noticed a change in my body. I went to my gynecologist and found out I was pregnant with our first child, Jammieon, Jr.! I called Jamie to tell him, and he was so excited he planned a trip to come back to visit me that March. While there, he asked me to marry him, and I said yes!

I knew my life was about to change forever by marrying into the military. My crew at work urged me to leave the job due to the tremendous amount of stress, so I put in my two weeks' notice at the end of April. Jamie had my things moved to South Dakota where he was stationed. I moved out and went to stay with my mother and grandmother in my hometown, Linden, AL. The wedding had been set for June 11th and I didn't want to shack up before marriage. I got to spend two months of quality time with my mom and grandmother. They tried to fatten me up and helped with planning the wedding and reception. My mother was so excited she was having her first grandchild, but she was sad I'd be moving so far away. The ceremony was held at my childhood church Unity Baptist and the reception at Demopolis Civic Center. Jamie rode the bus to AL for the wedding so we could drive my car back. He even got his hair cut by the local barber, Salt, for the wedding. The day after the wedding we loaded the car up and drove back to South Dakota. He had a beautiful split-level, three-bedroom, two-bath, and two-car garage house built in Box Elder, SD, for my wedding gift.

When we arrived in South Dakota, we began to move and unpack our things to get the house situated and ready for the baby. He and his brother were renting a home together prior to him having the house built. Once we got situated, I immediately began to look for work. I was around five to six months pregnant at this point. We were looking forward to being stationed at Ellsworth for four years. I wanted to work as much as I could to help bridge the gap in expenses and income. I decided to print my resume and take a copy to a few colleges in the area and colleges on the base in hopes of landing a teaching position after the baby came. I also reluctantly put in a resume at Sylvan Learning Center (SLC). This was a turning point for me, I believe. I have a bachelor's in math, a master's in applied math, and everything except the internship for Master of Education, and here I was applying for a job with hourly pay. Of course, this was the job that called me back. Since this was the only place I heard back from, I accepted and began to work as a tutor, tutoring geometry and algebra under my supervisor, Deanna. It was a fulfilling job helping students of all ages realize their potential, but the pay seemed low for someone with a master's degree.

I went in for my 38-week checkup and had high blood pressure, so Dr. Christensen sent me over to the hospital to be induced. I wasn't ready y'all! This was going to be my first childbirth, so I was terrified, especially since something seemed to be wrong!!!! Jamie took me to the hospital but had to leave because my go bag wasn't in the car. There was no one to come hold my hand or comfort me while he was gone, and the nurse was just awful. She made it seem like it was my fault that the baby was having to be induced. I was in tears and upset with no one to comfort me! As a first-time mom, what she said to me upset me just as much as the thought of something being wrong. One of the challenges of being a military spouse was being in a new place with no family and friends, having to rely solely on each other during the unexpected. Once admitted, I was given an IV to start the meds and some meds to help me sleep. I never actually went to sleep. When Jamie returned, he was asked to hold one of my legs for the birth. There were no stirrups. I knew this had to be traumatizing for him, but he did it. During the birth, a class walked by the room and asked to view. At this point, I didn't care—sure, come on in, the more the merrier. It took me two pushes, like a pro, and Jr. was out! My dad and mom arrived the next day to see their first grandson! I will never forget the look on their faces when they heard his middle name was my brother's, who died shortly after childbirth, making me an only child. They both stayed a while after Jr. was born. This would be my mom's only visit to South Dakota. I will tell you more about this later.

For a while, finances were tight. We had enough to pay the bills but stretched the last little bit to buy groceries. There were times when my mom would send us her leftover food stamps so we could fill our freezer to eat. I stayed humble and kept looking for jobs. I knew I could not do anything full time not knowing when or where the military would move us, but my long-term goal was to one day be a professor. I also didn't want to be away from my first child all day if I could help it. I finally stumbled across and applied for a tutoring job for South Dakota School of Mines and Technology (SDSM&T) that paid just as well as a teaching position. I went in for the interview and got the job! I mentioned the interview to my supervisor at Sylvan and to my surprise, one of the interview panelists was her mom. I believe she put in a good word for me. The job was based on a grant, so it would be temporary. This meant I would continue to inquire about positions at places where I had taken a resume until I was where I wanted to be, in a college classroom again.

I'd passed the boards for teaching grade school in AL but would have to take the Praxis to teach grade school in SD. I wasn't interested in teaching grade school, so I didn't bother to test in SD. I was an upper-level mathematics tutor, tutoring calculus and differential equations while at SDSM&T. I bet I could've passed the Praxis given my exposure to all math in this position, but I never gave it a thought. What's ironic is I tutored someone to take the Praxis on the side. I started out tutoring in the library. It was here I met two colleagues, Kelsey and Mike, who I am still friends with today. I was eventually given an office that I shared with another instructor, Jim Nelson. One day he asked me out for coffee. I thought it was weird, but I went with it. I chose the Starbucks in the mall to meet in a public place. When I met with him, he told me he was retiring but had been asked to teach at National American University (NAU). He said he turned down the offer but referred me instead!!! I could not believe it!!! I did not know what to say, especially since he went on to compliment me. I told him thank you and asked for the contact information. He told me her name was Gale Folsland and gave me her number. He had me call her right there while I was with him. She answered and we agreed on a date and time for me to come in for what I thought would be an interview. When I arrived, Gale asked me questions to get to know me, had me fill out some paperwork, and gave me my materials and schedule for my classes. Seems I had the job already just based on my referral!!! Getting the tutoring position at SDSM&T and position at NAU both taught me a lesson. It is not always what you know, but who you know, too. I also learned to be humble. You may not always start out in the job you want, but you can continue to make connections while working toward it. Things might have turned out differently if I allowed my pride to keep me from working at SLC as a tutor with a master's degree.

I began teaching on-ground for NAU right away while still tutoring for SDSM&T in the morning and tutoring for Sylvan on the weekends. I had gone from going to separate places with my resume to having three jobs that all worked out timewise. I worked at SDSM&T from 8-10 a.m., M-TH, then I had classes at NAU from 10 a.m.-12 p.m., M-TH, and I worked for Sylvan on the weekend. Not too long after all this, I was contacted by Black Hills State University (BHSU), a school on base I'd taken a resume to, to teach night classes. I accepted knowing that I would have to let something go, even though the times were going to work out teaching classes once a week at night from 7-10 p.m. I decided to let Sylvan go and continue to work at SDSM&T until the grant ran out. I was quickly learning that there were lots of job opportunities having a math degree in a military town where there was a lot of turnover and most did not wish to live. After I took the NAU position, I began to turn down positions so I wouldn't be overworked.

I made beneficial use of my time working on my lectures and materials for NAU and BHSU classes while at SDSM&T, when there were no students coming in for tutoring. I never had an office for my NAU and BHSU positions at the schools, so my husband made me one at home. This forced me to be creative with meeting with students and not bringing work home. I would meet with students before or after class if it wasn't a late class. I also stayed after, in the classroom I taught in, to do my grading or answer student questions, if class was done early. We didn't really have room for an office in the house, but we made the extra space in the HVAC and water heater closet work. It was big enough for my desk, a desktop computer with monitor and tower, printer, and file cabinet. He put some shelves up on the wall for my class folders and books to use all the space. It was noisy most of the time from the air conditioner, but it was a place I could go to work undisturbed; hey, it worked! I was able to make my own schedule, so Jamie was home with Jr. when I had to work.

My husband deployed for six months, twice, during our four-year term at Ellsworth AFB, spanning 2006–2010. When I found out about the first deployment, I called my mom to tell her and asked if she'd come stay with me while Jamie was gone to help with the baby. I was going to need someone to watch him while I was at work. She agreed, so I sent her a one-way bus ticket. In early December 2007, one month before Jamie's first deployment, my mom had a brain aneurysm. She was at her boyfriend's house, had a headache, and decided to take a nap. He happened to go in and check on her. When he walked in and turned on the light, her eyes were rolling back. He rushed her to Demopolis, AL, to the emergency room. When they got there, the doctor told him she had a brain aneurysm, and they were going to have to fly her to the hospital in Birmingham, AL. I don't remember who called to tell me what happened, but as soon as I heard, I was making plans to get there. It was around finals time for my classes, so I printed my finals and asked my colleague, Mike, if he would administer the test for me. After I explained the situation, he graciously agreed. Next, I called and told my husband, and asked him to see if he could get leave to go too. I was surprised he was able to take time, but glad he was going to be accompanying me.

Jamie, Jr., and I hopped on a flight the next day. Luckily, Jr. was only eighteen months, so his seat was free. I made sure to grab Christmas photos we'd taken at Wal-Mart to take to my mom. When we arrived in Birmingham, both my best friends were there, Cynthia and Berinda, along with some of my mom's siblings, Rosa and Isadore. I greeted everyone but was more concerned with going back to see my mom. I couldn't take Jr. back into the NICU due to the germs, but Jamie and my aunt went back with me. As soon as I saw her, this feeling that she wasn't going to make it washed over me and I burst into tears! There was a patch on the right side of her head shaved, with a tube coming out to drain the blood to relieve the pressure on her brain. My aunt told me not to cry, to be strong. This upset me. Why do I have to be strong now seeing my mom in this state? I finally got myself together to go in and speak to her. I'd taken the Christmas pictures back to show her, hoping they would lift her spirits. She didn't remember I was married, so she didn't recognize Jamie. She didn't remember her first grandson, so she didn't remember Jr. It was so sad. She had memory loss from the aneurysm. I made sure to hug her and tell her I loved her before we left her room. Somewhere deep down, I felt this would be my last time seeing her alive.

When we got to our hotel room, I talked to Jamie about staying. I didn't want to leave her. Jamie asked where we would stay and when we would be home. I didn't really know. All I knew was I wanted to stay. He told me I needed to come home and take care of my family, so I left. I went back to work and gave the finals myself. After a few days, I got a call late at night from the doctor that my mom probably wouldn't make it through the night. I called my dad to book me and Jr. a flight. I didn't bother asking Jamie to see if he could get leave. I knew he wouldn't be able to since it wasn't his mom. When we landed at our connection in Utah around 10 a.m., I called my uncle Alfred to get an update. He told me all was well and have a safe trip. When I landed in Birmingham, I was picked up from the airport and taken directly to the hospital. When I walked in, my uncle Alfred took Jr. and told me she was gone! I wailed, crying as loud as I could with all the hurt in my heart. My uncle Alfred and Isadore embraced me until I calmed down. The decision was made without me to pull the plug on my mother before I'd arrived.

Her time of death was around the time I was in Utah. They didn't want to tell me because I was traveling alone with Jr., but also didn't wait until I got there. I don't think I will ever forget that.

After I calmed down, I asked to see her body, but Abernathy Funeral Home had already come to get her. This was another shock and blow to my heart, not being able to see her one last time. We all got in the car and drove to Linden to begin making funeral arrangements. She needed a wig for burial given her state in the hospital. I wanted to make the program since she'd just helped me with the program for my wedding. I wanted to dress her in white with her Elks Lodge Daughter collar to honor her membership in the organization. My mom didn't have insurance, so we had to raise money for the funeral. Her siblings each helped with the cost. I received generous donations from my sorority sisters of Zeta Phi Beta Sorority, Inc., Theta Beta Chapter of Tuskegee University. I received donations and support from Linden High School class of 1998, with multiple classmates attending the funeral. The next time I would see her after leaving the hospital would be at the wake. She'd be embalmed with skin hard to the touch when I went to kiss her. Nonetheless, I felt like Abernathy Funeral Home did a wonderful job.

The next day at the funeral, I was happy to see family, friends, my dad, his siblings, my classmates, the Elks Lodge, and my stepdad. We walked to the front pew on the left side of the church and sat. After all the family was seated, the viewing of the body for everyone else started. Each person came by to embrace me as they walked back to find a seat. I was holding it together until the last person hugged me, her best friend, Ruth Dill. By this time, my dad had grabbed Jr. When she hugged me, a flood of sadness washed over me, and I wept on her shoulder as they closed the casket on my mom, never to be opened again. The service was nice with family, friends, and Elks Lodge members all speaking highly of Mom. The only part of the service I wasn't happy about was the eulogy. I felt our pastor said things that he could've kept to himself, especially having no knowledge. She was buried in the family cemetery and the reception was at Linden Elementary lunchroom. Lots of people expressed their condolences while also expressing their displeasure with the pastor. I won't name him here, but if I ever get a chance to, I will tell him where he was wrong and how he made us all feel. When we returned home, I told Jamie I would never forgive him for making me come home to take care of my family while my mother was in the NICU. He apologized, understanding that I would never get that time back. I realized in that moment that he and Jr. were my family now that I was married. It was a hard pill to swallow, but a true realization in that moment. I am glad I got to spend the time I did with her while I was pregnant, after I left Anheuser-Busch, and planning the wedding. Two milestones she could rest well knowing she didn't miss. She was at peace!

My husband had three people volunteer to take his place for the upcoming deployment in January so he could stay home with his wife in mourning, but he was still sent. This left me with little faith in the military that they cared about families as a military spouse. No wonder the divorce rate was so high amongst the military. Since my plan for my mom to come and help with Jr. was no longer a possibility, my cousin, Lajoye, transferred her Walmart job to South Dakota and stayed with me until I found daycare for Jr. This was amazing! It was great having her there! I began the search for a daycare or babysitter for Jr. I don't remember how I found her, but I landed on a lady running an affordable daycare out of her home near ours for $80/week. It was hard leaving my child with a stranger, but it was my only choice with no family nearby. Since this was my first child and I was breastfeeding, it was exceptionally hard to be separated. The time away from the baby turned out to be refreshing. She was even nice enough to come pick him up a few weekends while Jamie was deployed to give me a break! She had no idea how amazing this was! I kept myself so busy working while Jamie was gone there was no time to mourn my mother's passing. This would catch up with me later.

Communicating with Jamie was slim. He had two 15-minute phone calls a week where he would call by patching through to the base or by phone card, so anything that needed to be discussed had to be kept in a list format for me to remember and get through it. We were so happy when he came home! There is nothing like seeing your loved one come home after a deployment; however, I had to adjust to him being home. I was used to the house being clean and organized, only having to pick up after myself and Jr. I was used to being able to grab a bite for me and Jr. and not cook. It took a while, but we soon got in a groove and began personalizing our first home by landscaping and putting up a fence.

During the second deployment, we kept in touch through Yahoo messenger messaging and video, back when Logitech cameras had to be added to your desktop. We found out about a month before he returned that we'd be making a permanent change of station (PCS) to Wichita Falls, Texas. Jamie was going to be a technical school instructor! This came at a time when I had two positions that I didn't want to leave. Two of the challenges of being a military spouse are having to move when you've found a wonderful job with great colleagues and having to look for new employment. I went online to do a search for colleges in the area. I found four: Embry Riddle, Wayland Baptist, Midwestern State University, and Vernon College. I went to Midwestern State and Vernon College websites and applied to teach. I didn't want to wait until we arrived to hand deliver resumes like I did in South Dakota. I heard back from Midwestern first. I was told they had a good math teacher, so there was no interest for me. Vernon College asked me to contact them when we were moved and settled. Sounded like a prospect to me, one that I was excited about because I could teach on the base.

Next, I went to each of my supervisors to break the news that I'd be moving soon and could no longer work. To my surprise, my supervisor at NAU wanted me to remain with NAU. She asked me to get in touch with Andrea Serna if I was interested in teaching online. I jumped at the opportunity! I let her know we were moving in February and asked if I could have a little time to settle in before classes were assigned to me. My supervisor at BHSU was extremely sad to hear the news. I was teaching four night classes at the time, Monday through Thursday, each from 7-10 p.m., and one more class would've been full time. She would basically be losing a full-time instructor in an area where math teachers were hard to come by. I felt bad but moving wasn't a choice with the military. Since NAU offered and I never knew they had online classes, I figured I'd ask if BHSU had online classes. Unfortunately, they did not. To this day, I am still friends on Facebook with some adults that took my classes while in South Dakota; Rebecca, Cheryl, and Dawn. Their success and fulfillment are why I teach!

Jamie arrived back from his second deployment on Jan 29, 2010. Since we were so close, we decided to take a trip to Colorado before moving to Texas. We were also selling the house to leave for Texas at the same time, given the fast turnaround. We only had a few weeks to sell since we were scheduled to be in Texas mid-February. One of the things on our itinerary when we arrived in Winter Park was skiing lessons. We got dressed in all our rental gear, headed out to the slopes, and I almost fainted. This was not happening today, but we did get a picture in the gear. The rental company was nice enough to refund us our money for the rental and the class. They educated us that we needed to acclimate to the altitude before doing physical activities such as skiing. We had no idea, of course. We did enjoy the rest of the trip! We went shopping, went on a dinner sleigh ride, and attended a Denver Nuggets game where they played against one of my favorite teams, the San Antonio Spurs!!!! While we were away, we got an offer on the house and were able to complete paperwork through our resort office!! We were ready for the move.

We got to Wichita Falls, TX, March 2010, got settled into base housing, and I had my first set of classes offered the same month. I was ready for the challenge of trying something new with online instruction. Even though I was teaching online with NAU, I still decided to contact Vernon College for a sit down. When we arrived in Wichita Falls, we traded our two vehicles in for one, to save money since I'd be working from home. I was told by Vernon College the classes would be at night on base. This would work for us given my husband worked during the day, so I was willing to try it. During the meeting, I learned the classes would be moved to the campus in town. Since I was already teaching online for the college I was working for on-ground, I decided to let this opportunity go, even though it paid a little more than online classes. By the time I bought gas and work clothes, not to mention keeping my hair up and writing new lectures, it just didn't seem worth it to me. I feel like they missed an opportunity not hiring me before I arrived, especially since NAU offered me to continue with them online.

The lightheadedness continued, so when we got to Sheppard I went to the doctor. Turns out we were pregnant with our second child, Dantonio. It wasn't the altitude at all. It was fresh back from deployment loving! We were excited that Jammieon, Jr. would finally have a sibling! Since Jamie deployed six months on and six months off after we married, it was difficult to try for another. Here we are four years later, getting ready to have our second child at thirty. While pregnant with Toni, I was an insomniac. I'd stay up all night and then finally get sleepy when Jamie was leaving for work. I'd be up watching the Food Network, learning new recipes to try, playing online poker on the PlayStation, or getting my work done in my online classes. One night, I was super uncomfortable and kept feeling like I needed to go to the bathroom. Jamie got up and went to work as usual while I got up and took a shower to try and relax. As I got out of the tub, I fell to my knees in pain! Luckily, I'd taken the phone in the bathroom with me, so I called the doctor. They asked if my contractions were five minutes apart. They weren't, so the doctor told me to stay home. I hung up, called Jamie at work, and told him to get home, I was about to have the baby. One of his co-worker's wives met us at the hospital after picking Jr. up from school for us.

When we arrived at the hospital, they checked me, and I was dilated ten centimeters!!!! If I'd stayed at home, I would've had Toni there. If I'd called Jamie just a few minutes later, he would've been away from his phone. Since Dr. Godfrey had told me to stay home, he still gave me my epidural even though I was ten centimeters. I was so grateful because at this point, the pain was real! There was an anesthesiologist giving me an epidural, while a nurse gave me an IV, and another was drawing blood to get me ready as Toni was crowning already!!! It literally took one push and Toni was welcomed to the world! He was born in October 2010, just a few months after we arrived in TX. We had to stay in the hospital in a family room a few extra days, through Halloween, due to Toni being jaundiced. It took an emotional toll on me until he was ok. Even though I didn't have time off, it didn't affect me when he came. I could easily login to my courses on a laptop while in the hospital without missing a beat! I really appreciated this convenience. Having an online teaching position also afforded me the choice to stay home with Dantonio until he was eligible for school! This brought me so much joy! He never had to see the inside of a daycare, unlike our first child, Jr.

Being a stay-at-home mom (SAHM) while working online did get rough at times with the addition of a second kid. Having the ability to multitask early on in life would really pay off juggling two kids, a job, and a household. My office was set up in the living room, so I could work whenever I had time each day. It took me about six months to get into a new routine after Toni arrived though. I was breastfeeding him, so I had to find time to get dressed, rest, cook, clean, sleep, and spend time with my husband in between feedings. This was exhausting but rewarding at the same time! Not having family around to help me, I began to appreciate the role my grandmother played in helping my mom raise me. For a military family, this was an all-too-familiar challenge, having kids with no family or extended family around to help raise them. Jr. had started pre-K at Sheppard Elementary in August after we arrived in TX, so this helped. I was starting to want to get out of the house more. I never really got out much on the base when we were in South Dakota to make friends. I'd meet people when Jamie had them over for poker games. Usually, if I made a new friend, Denise, my hairdresser while in South Dakota, would be the one to introduce me.

I got an invite to a BeautiControl Spa one day while picking Jr. up from school, so I decided to go. The spa was relaxing, and I liked the products, so I ended up signing up to join. This was my way to get out of the house and meet new people.

We'd pay as a group to do events, ask passersby to be hosts, and show our products in a spa-based presentation complete with facial, relaxation, hand massage, and foot treatment. While I was successful with sales, I was never able to build a team to get to the next level being in such a small market. I kept a separate account so I could keep track of if I was making money or not. I earned a Tiffany necklace, mug, jewelry box, purses, and a cruise through sales, but I never built a successful team, which was hard to do in all MLMs (multi-level marketing). I wouldn't recommend this as a profession. It did serve its purpose in getting me out of the house. I traveled all over TX to Electra, Quanah, Iowa Park, Burkburnett, Olney, Graham, and Vernon for spas, Dallas for conferences, and Memphis, TN, for retreats. Conferences and retreats were fun! I got to meet even more people while attending professional development seminars that not only helped me in BeautiControl but also with NAU. I gained lifelong friends from BeautiControl who I keep in touch with. I began to listen to CDs and read books by the likes of Simon Sinek and Jim Rohn for professional development. Later, I also began sessions with a life coach, Pam. She helped me work through my mom's death at a retreat and we continued that work plus professional development afterward. I won't spend much time on this time in my life and wrap it up here. I learned that all people you meet and connect with aren't meant to continue with you on your journey. You must learn in life to let people go, especially when they have shown you who they are.

I struggled a bit with being a SAHM and an online instructor after we moved. Because we never knew where the military would take us, I knew my best bet was to work as an adjunct part time. If I wanted to apply for a full-time position, I would need a PhD to be on a tenure track. Even though I had a career where I was able to stay home and raise my beautiful family, I didn't feel successful. When I joined Facebook, I was able to reconnect and follow my roommates, friends, and classmates from high school and college. This was a blessing and a curse. I was able to see how all their careers were flourishing in success while I was moving around as a military spouse. During a conversation with my college roommate, Stephanie, I mentioned my feelings of being unsuccessful to her. She had an interesting perspective. She told me people are successful in diverse ways. She also told me she wished she had the time with her kids that I did. I never thought anyone would look at my life in comparison as I did theirs. This is where I learned comparison is the thief of joy! If I had any advice to give, it'd be to walk your own path. Learn to be happy with where you are presently while working on your future self. Life goals should be being a better version of yourself the next day, not being like someone else. You have no idea what people are going through or went through to be where they are, and it really is none of your business either. Living life this way gives you a sense of freedom over your life to be unapologetically you.

I also struggled with my sinuses when we moved to TX. We thought it was due to mold that was found under the carpet in our first base house. The A/C was leaking onto the carpet and caused mold, so we were moved from our three bedroom to a four bedroom. The move did help, but I was still having issues with multiple sinus infections. This was beginning to affect my ability to work during the day. I'd need to take headache meds to try and sleep the pain off before everyone was home. Luckily, Toni would want to sleep too. I went to the doctor multiple times before finding the right mix of sinus meds to give me some relief! Then in late 2011, we found out we were expecting our third son, Kalob! We'd tried for a girl and ended up with another boy! The move couldn't have come at a better time! Everyone would be able to have their own room and we'd still have a guestroom for any visitors. We set my office up in the laundry room with shelves above my desk for space and I made it work. The pregnancy was as it was with both his brothers, Jr. and Toni. There was no morning sickness, but there was back pain. I ended up going to see a chiropractor, Dr. Cartwright, who helped tremendously! I am still a patient, seeing him once a month for maintenance.

Kalob was born in September 2012. That evening, my Braxton-Hicks were getting closer and closer, so we called a friend of mine at the time in BeautiControl, Jennifer, who'd offered to come over and stay with the other boys when it was time. We got to the hospital and there were three other women that arrived at the same time in labor and delivery. I was checked, told I was dilated six centimeters, and asked if I wanted an epidural. I said yes and waited for the anesthesiologist to arrive. He came in and did his thing. A while after he was gone, I told Jamie I wasn't feeling much of any relief. Dr. Horth then walked in and said it was time to push. She wiped chlorohexidine down below and I felt it! She was like, 'I guess the epidural didn't take, but it is time to push.' This, of course, frightened and upset me at the same time, but I was able to push him out after two pushes!!! Our baby boy was here! We had to stay in the hospital a bit because he had jaundice, but I didn't have to worry about time off from the job because I could log on from anywhere. I was also able to breastfeed Kalob because I worked from home. I had about the same adjustment period with Kalob as I did Toni, six months, but let me tell you, having two at home and one in school while working was a new challenge. I'd have to try and get them both to sleep to work or get Toni, who was a little older, to entertain Kalob while I worked. But it all worked out.

In 2014, during force reshaping, Jamie decided to retire early at sixteen years with full benefits. After several interviews, he decided to take a contracting job on base in the same squadron he was in before retiring. After finding a job and deciding to make Wichita Falls our home, we began searching for a house with our realtor, Ricardo. Base housing had only given us a few months to move so we didn't have much time. We looked at every four bedroom there was for two weeks before finally settling on our second home. It was in an older, more mature neighborhood, in town, with great schools walking distance away. We loved the space inside, the yard, and how the master bedroom was on a separate side from the kids' rooms. We knew we wanted to build a shed and garage, the house only had a two-car carport, so we got right to making the home ours. Everyone had their own rooms, but we ended up putting Kalob and Toni in bunkbeds in one of the Jack and Jill rooms and Jr. in the other. They didn't want to be in a room alone. This worked out, giving us an extra room for a guestroom and my office.

We kept Jr. in school on the base and were able to get Toni in school on base too for kindergarten. They'd ride to school with their dad, and I'd pick them up. In the fall of 2015, we got word that the contractor Jamie was working for, Advanced Concepts, lost the contract, and Jamie was going to have to look for new employment. This news was incredibly stressful, especially since now we had a mortgage to pay, but it worked out. The new contractor, Patch Plus, kept all the earlier contracted employees. I guess retired life was sweet because at the end of 2015, we found out we were pregnant with our fourth. The boys were hoping this would be a girl, but I knew it was another boy! During our Facebook reveal video, complete with team boy and team girl t-shirts, we found out we were having another boy, Keshawn! Our family was about to grow yet again! We were back at ease, thinking surely this contract would last more than a year, only to be in the same situation a year later during the pregnancy. This time, we decided to take a different approach because we realized the contracts on base were always going to be unstable. Jamie started looking for other opportunities. He applied and got an interview with Siemens in Chicago set for August 24, 2016. He also applied and got an offer for a yearlong contract position overseas in Saudi. Jamie never made it to the interview in Chicago. Keshawn decided to come an entire month early, just days before the interview, so Siemens gave the job to someone else. Given the circumstances surrounding his birth, Jamie decided not to take the job offer in Saudi either.

I remember August 22, 2016, like yesterday. It was the first day of the 2016-2017 school year for Wichita Falls ISD. This was Dantonio's first year of school. He was starting kindergarten and Jr. was starting fourth grade. I took a shower, got dressed, and made a protein shake before I drove Jr. and Dantonio to school. I had office hours on Zoom when I returned home. Even though Dantonio had been home with me his whole life, he was like Jr. his first day of school, ready to go! This helped with the anxiety of leaving my child at school. I completed my work during my office hours and went into our room to rest. I noticed the baby hadn't been moving much, so I called my obstetrician's office. They told me to drink OJ to see if I could get the baby moving. I did and didn't notice much of a change. Later in the afternoon, I began to have bad Braxton-Hicks contractions. I still managed to drive and pick Jr. and Toni up from school, but by the time Jamie got home, I was over the contractions. He told me to call the doctor's office again. I called and the doctor told me to eat some dinner and sit down and rest. We ate dinner, I sat down to rest again, but I was still having Braxton-Hicks and not a whole lot of movement. I told Jamie we needed to head to the hospital because the baby was coming early. He couldn't believe this was happening now, days before he was to leave for his interview, but I was sure this baby was coming and I needed to get to the hospital.

I called my friend, Latoya, to see if she could come by to sit with the boys until the babysitter, Kari, got there. She said sure and headed on over. As soon as she arrived, we headed to the hospital. When we got there, I was checked and admitted. I was around five to six centimeters. Jamie let the nurses know that I wanted an epidural as they hooked up the baby monitor. We sat there in the room for a while before the doctor arrived. I'd been breathing through the contractions. When Dr. Moore arrived, she said the cord was around the baby's neck and I wouldn't be able to get an epidural due to his pulse. This upset Jamie something fierce. I tried to remain as calm as I could, having experienced a somewhat natural childbirth with Kalob since the epidural didn't take. The doctor then told us if my water didn't break, I'd have to have a C-section. I saw the anger in Jamie's eyes turn to concern. At that exact moment, I looked at him, my water broke, and the doctor told me it was time to push. There was no time to scream and cry, my baby boy was in distress, so I pushed as hard as I could, almost to the point of passing out. The doctor told me to take one more push, so I squeezed Jamie's hand and pushed as hard as I could again. Keshawn was born at 8:25 p.m. at 4 lbs. 9 oz and 17 inches long at 36 weeks.

Jamie burst into tears when he arrived. We got a glance at him before they took him off to the nursery to clean him. The nurses took me to a room to get me cleaned up. Then, we walked down to the nursery to see Keshawn. His dad noticed he'd stopped breathing! We called a nurse over, they massaged his chest to get him breathing, and put him on oxygen. He'd spend over two and a half weeks in the hospital on oxygen with a feeding tube after his birth. I was discharged and went up to the hospital every three hours to deliver breastmilk and feed him. I wanted to be there for every feeding I could to get his weight up for discharge. It was an exhausting and stressful task along with work, having two other kids in school, and general house duties, but we wanted him home as soon as possible. He came home during Labor Day weekend, and we were thrilled. He started breastfeeding, no more tubes or bottles, after he arrived at home and never took another bottle for over two years!

    A contractor friend told Jamie to apply for a position with Lockheed Martin overseas. He did, was selected for a phone interview, and got the job! He flew out to South Carolina for orientation with a leave date of January 2017, five months after Keshawn's birth. The contract was for a year. He'd have a room, transportation, security, and meals provided, so all he needed to take was clothes and entertainment. It was going to be a sacrifice to be away that long, so we sat down and talked about what our goals were for the money. Since now even this house was going to end up being too little for our family, the plan was to use the money to buy our forever home and land. We didn't want to be in a neighborhood where your neighbor was right beside you, as we really kept to ourselves. I worked from home, took care of our finances, took the kids to school, and helped them with their work. Since I had a breastfeeding newborn, I needed a yard guy. I wouldn't be able to leave the baby in the house to cut the grass, plus I am allergic to the grass here in TX. I had Jamie buy a set of clippers so I could cut the boys' hair, so we were all set. Even though I had no family here, I knew if I got in a real pinch there were friends I'd be able to call. Let me shout out to a few of those friends here. One friend came in clutch giving me breaks and helping when and where she could while Jamie was deployed, Kendra Bowser. There were others that helped by bringing things by and coming by Latoya, Kendra Burley, Lisa, and Susan. Anna introduced me to Thrive, which helped me physically. Berinda and Kasey helped keep me mentally stable being there to listen. It's good to have friends that are therapists!

It was sad when Jamie left, but this time we were able to keep in touch through Facebook messenger. We were able to make video calls, so he could see the kids. Since it was the second semester of the kids' school year, we were able to stay in a good routine. I'd wake up, get Toni and Jr. ready for school, load all the boys in the van, drop Toni and Jr. at school, come home, feed Kalob and Keshawn, turn on Kalob's shows, put Keshawn to sleep, grab a protein shake, and then settle down to work. Once work was done, I'd feed the kids lunch, watch a show while on the treadmill, grab a shower, get dressed, and load the van to pick up the other two from school. Once they were home from school, we ate dinner and then completed homework. I gave them a few hours to play and then it was bath time. I'd cut their hair every two weeks on the weekend, so I wouldn't have to add this during the week.

Not even a month into his deployment, Jamie called me and told me a fire destroyed all his belongings in his room. My heart dropped but he wasn't in the room at the time of the fire. That was all that mattered to me. He was ok. He was in good spirits even though he lost everything saying the things could be replaced. He gave me a list of things he lost and/or needed. He told me the company would set up a way for me to get the items to him considering no mail was allowed, but this was a special case. A friend, Lisa, was nice enough to sit with the kids while I ran around collecting the items he needed. He later told me the company would cover the cost for the items lost. This was unexpected but appreciated!

Not long after this incident, a huge health development arose with Keshawn. I took Keshawn to his first well baby visit and things seemed to be going well. It was at his second well check at six months when there was a concern. I noticed his right eye would wander to the right, so I mentioned it to the doctor. She told me it was normal at that age, and we'd keep an eye on it. He did, however, show delayed development, so I was given a referral for physical and occupational therapy. It took a few months to get in for an evaluation and we didn't get on the schedule afterward until September 2017. He'd have PT and OT appointments on the same day, 2–3 times a week. Keshawn was not a fan of therapy, so he'd scream almost the entire time. It was incredibly hard to watch, but I got through by telling myself it was necessary. I had to quickly learn to take it one day at a time and not stress about the future. I'd make the appointments during the day so I could go while Toni and Jr. were at school, taking Kalob with me. It was exhausting at times, but progress was being made.

At his nine-month well visit, his eye was still wandering, so I asked for a referral to see an ophthalmologist. I set up an appointment for September 12, 2017, with Dr. Packwood, once the referral came through. Since the appointment was two hours away in Southlake, TX, I booked it for 10 a.m. This would give me enough time to drop Toni and Jr. off at school. The appointment was estimated to be two hours because he'd need to be dilated. Of course, Keshawn was not having drops in his eyes, so I had to hold him down while they pried his eyes open. This was incredibly traumatic for him and I. After waiting thirty minutes, the doctor examined Keshawn's eyes. He then gave me the news that Keshawn was severely nearsighted and needed glasses. He recommended I get an MRI of his brain as soon as possible and booked his next open appointment at Cook Children's Medical Center to test him for glaucoma on October 31, 2017. The glasses were too expensive from their office, so I didn't buy them there. Tricare didn't cover frames or lenses. I got in the car and burst into tears. I was filled with emotions, wondering what was wrong with my little boy. I still had to get us a bite to eat before driving back and picking the boys up from school, so I had to pull myself together. I planned to research eyewear places, take Keshawn to get glasses, and call his primary care manager to ask for a neurologist referral.

The next day, I took Keshawn to Eye Mart Express in Wichita Falls to get his glasses. I found a cute light blue frame with a head strap in the back to keep them on. The frame and the lenses were super expensive even with a teacher discount. He needed them, so I got them. Little did I know, a long relationship with this establishment would ensue. I got the neurologist referral and set up an appointment with Dr. Al Rifai in Frisco, TX, yet another 2-hour drive away. He examined Keshawn and set up an appointment for an MRI for 11:25 a.m. on October 12, 2017, at Allen Presby Hospital which was over two and a half hours away. Keshawn would need to be put to sleep for the MRI, so it would need to be done at a hospital that specialized in pediatric MRIs. The same situation applied. I would drop the boys at school and drive to the appointment. If anything went wrong, the only person I could count on at the school to watch or take the boys home was Mrs. Hooper, a teacher at the kids' school I was good friends with. We arrived for the appointment, and I was so nervous. Keshawn had been on oxygen after birth when he stopped breathing, so I was afraid something would happen. The staff were all amazing, so much so that Keshawn seemed to be relaxed. When they wheeled him out to set up his IV and anesthesia, I posted on Facebook for the first time what I'd been going through. There was an outpouring of support! When Keshawn was done, I was called back to sit with him as he awakened. I was so relieved! He ate and drank nicely, so we were able to leave soon after.

I was nervous on the drive home, checking to make sure he was breathing and not having any complications after the MRI. I made it back in time to get the boys from school. The neurologist had already set up an appointment to get the results of the MRI, so I drove back to Frisco, TX. The neurologist said Keshawn had Congenital CMV Cytomegalovirus. I'd never heard of it before. We had three other boys with no other issues at birth besides jaundice. He told us Keshawn would need physical and occupational therapy through the age of sixteen. Again, this was another blow that left me in tears when I reached the car.

I was glad to finally know what was going on, but this brought so many more worries with all the possibilities with this diagnosis. Keshawn already needed glasses, but he could have hearing loss. Keshawn was already in PT and OT, so I didn't need referrals, but I still needed to see his primary care manager, Dr. Kofron. I made an appointment to see her, and I will never forget her telling me Keshawn may never walk. I cried in the car. When I went to his next PT appointment, I talked with his therapist, Lindsey, about the diagnosis and about what the doctor said. She clarified that the doctor was giving me the worst case and Keshawn may be able to walk with aid. This made me feel a little better, but there was a long road of therapy ahead including years of six appointments per week for PT, OT, and eventually speech. He began to do a modified crawl in PT where he dragged his legs, and he began to eat with his hands and a spoon in OT. His physical therapists, Kristen, Lou, and Amanda, and his occupational therapist, Abby, Rachel, and Zack, were so proud! He never really talked to his speech therapist, Natasha, but he talked all the time at home. I'd take her video when I could catch him.

I had to switch from daytime appointments to evening appointments during his therapy and got to see more children that were disabled. I empathized for the families and realized how much worse things could be for Keshawn; loss of hearing, blindness, immobility, inability to speak, and so much more. At this point, Jamie had been overseas two extra months, so it was March 2018. When I talked to Jamie on Facebook messenger, I sobbed, overwhelmed with feelings of sadness and exhaustion. I was grieving Keshawn's condition all over again it seemed. He told me to keep holding on. The next day, he told me he'd bought a ticket to come home for a visit for two weeks. It was a surprise because I always bought his ticket to come home when he could. He said he could see that I needed him. While he was home, Jamie went to inquire about a position he'd applied for on Sheppard AFB in his old squadron. A physical exam on Sheppard AFB was a pre-requisite for the position, so he had it done while visiting. If he hadn't come home due to my breakdown, he would've never been here to get the physical exam for the position on the base. He was able to get everything done to apply within a day of going back to Iraq and found out he got the position when he returned. I felt it was God's timing because it was the same position he worked in before retirement and loved. He wanted to complete another four months in Iraq because every four months they received a bonus, so he'd need to stay until May.

While my husband was in Iraq, I found out NAU had launched a ranking program, and given certain qualifications, you could apply for assistant professor, associate professor, or professor. Because my supervisors didn't really know me due to a high turnover rate, I found out about this program years after it was launched. When I decided to apply, I'd been an online instructor for eight years and employed with NAU for ten, counting my two years on-ground. I asked my current supervisor, I don't remember her name, for a recommendation and the application. Again, there had always been a high turnover rate with my supervisors, so asking my current one for help completing my application wasn't a thought in my mind and I don't remember her offering. The turnover rate was so bad I'd learned to do what I'd need a supervisor to do so I wouldn't need to depend on anyone to do my job. I'd like to also add, in all this time working for NAU, I never had or was assigned a mentor and never had an evaluation. I began to think who could help me with this endeavor. I called my classmate, Charles, who is an instructor at Alabama A&M. I talked with him about the requirements and ultimately asked him to write me a recommendation letter. I called my dad, who worked for Georgia Pacific, and his brother Robert, who worked in the Tuscaloosa school system as a principal, to help me with my personal statement. I sent all the materials needed at the time, which if I remember correctly were a referral from my supervisor, resume, all quarter credit hours taught, professional development, personal statement, letter of recommendation, and peer and student reviews. I never heard a word back. While I felt this was unprofessional, I just figured I didn't get the promotion and kept it moving. This changed my outlook on the job over the next few years. I was in a state where I didn't care if I received a contract or not each quarter but didn't want to put in a resignation. I felt unappreciated and neglected after taking on a contract every quarter for the last eight years and only ever turning down one.

Jamie was scheduled to return from Iraq Memorial Day weekend. I'd casually been searching online for a five-bedroom home, trying to find our forever home. I found a house that checked most of the boxes for what we wanted. I didn't really care for the pictures online, so I called my realtor, Ricardo, and asked him to set up a viewing. The drive out to the house seemed like we were in the middle of nowhere, and then this beautiful neighborhood opened across from a golf course. We drove down a little farther and turned into a beautiful neighborhood. I already loved how much the houses were spaced out. The house sat on a one and a half-acre lot. After looking inside, I wanted to put in an offer; mind you, I hadn't applied for a loan or put my house up for sale yet. There were four bedrooms with a big bonus room, three and a half bathrooms, each with a jetted tub, office, pantry, laundry, room for a theater, master suite, all other bedrooms upstairs, privacy-fenced backyard with concrete patio, gorgeous finishings, and a wooden shed out back with room for more.

My realtor told me there was already an offer on the house, but the sellers were open to more offers. I told him I wanted to use a local bank. He had a contact, so he set me up with a local bank loan officer to get me preapproved. I went in with the strongest offer I could knowing there was another offer on the table. The sellers countered. Since I went in with the strongest offer I could, I countered with the same offer. I told our realtor if it is for us, we'd get it. If not, we'd keep looking. He called me and told me they accepted!!! I was ecstatic, but in panic mode at the same time. I was about to buy a house but hadn't sold my own. Heck, it wasn't even on the market! I also realized I was about to have to pack up the house all on my own. My realtor said, "Now that you have found a house you like, we can focus on selling yours." He had some clients in mind that he'd like to bring by to see the house on Saturday. This only gave me two days to clean up, but I agreed under one condition. We didn't have to leave. He brought the couple by, and they stayed for like forty-five minutes. When they left, my realtor called and told me they planned to put an offer in on Monday after exploring insurance options. Sure enough, on Monday while I was completing my office hours, he sent me the offer on messenger. I accepted and he never had to list my house! Just like that! BOOM! Our growing family would be able to move and have the space we needed.

I kept Jamie in the loop on everything. DocuSign was a godsend. Jamie was set to arrive Friday, May 25th. I'd packed almost the entire house. I had some friends come by to help and donate boxes. I'd rented a U-Haul scheduled to pick up May 26th and return on May 28th. My friend, Donella and her family, along with a few of Jamie's co-workers, would be the MVPs here, helping finish packing, loading, and unloading the U-Haul. I'd booked us a hotel to stay in until signing day. I'd set up to sign documents to sell our house and buy the new house on May 30th. I'd even set up a family vacation to South Padre Island leaving May 31st for a week for some R&R. Your girl was a planning fool! Everything went smoothly! When Jamie drove the U-Haul to the house, it was his first time seeing it and he said I did good. We unloaded everything into the garage until we got back from vacation. When we got back from vacation on June 8th, we only had that weekend to move essential items inside the house. Jamie would start work that Monday, June 11th. Right back to business as usual.

Two months before the move, I'd gotten a new supervisor at NAU. She'd only be around for six months. The one thing I remember during her tenure was NAU went completely virtual. This would turn out to be a great move prior to the outbreak of COVID-19. Once this supervisor moved on, I received my current supervisor, Autumn, in January 2019. When she came on, a whole new administration did as well. They were eager to change the university for the better. Through surveys sent out, seemingly quarterly, I was able to express my concerns over the years.

A year and a half in as my new supervisor, she sent me an email saying that she would like to do an evaluation in August 2020. This brought on anxiety because I'd never had a formal evaluation, part of it was self-evaluation, and all four kids were home schooling due to COVID-19. My first supervisor, Andrea, sent me a quarterly evaluation based off my student reviews, but nothing formal for my human resources file. Since I didn't really know my new supervisor, I asked my husband and my Soror, Kenya, to help me with my submission of a self-evaluation.

My professional development at the time was either faculty development or mandatory training. I hadn't attended any conferences or heard of any. I ended up getting one exceed, three meets, and one below expectations. I was not happy about the below expectations rating. I received below expectations due to not putting feedback in the gradebook. This was something I wasn't aware I could do. Also, not having an announcement each week. The policy of my previous supervisor was to post an announcement through week 3 for added students, and by then, all students would have access to weekly emails. In our meeting after my submission and her review, I asked my supervisor if she could show me how to add feedback to the gradebook. She shared her screen and showed me while on our Zoom call, and I have been doing it ever since! I even created a gradebook feedback bank to house my most used responses. I told her why I only posted announcements through week 3 and said I'd post weekly in the future. I appreciated her willingness to help. I asked her if I could speak candidly and told her about my frustrations with the university, one of which was completing a packet for faculty ranking and never hearing anything back. I dropped the names of my supervisor's supervisor and the provost at the time; I remembered their names but didn't use them here. She told me they'd been let go, so the documents were probably never received! It made so much sense. I had become so self-sufficient I didn't even notice I didn't have a supervisor and was doing it all on my own.

I was so glad to get my first evaluation out of the way, but the below expectations left a bad taste. I would work on all things discussed to be better next evaluation, but I had bigger fish to fry. My husband and I had decided to keep all four boys home for the first grading period of Fall 2020 due to the outbreak of COVID-19. He was an essential employee, so he wasn't here during the day to help, and I was teaching three classes online. I was concerned with my kids' health while overlooking my mental health. Jammieon, Jr. had to login and complete work for all six of his classes daily. I thought he was responsible enough to handle it, but he became overwhelmed and needed help. I helped him form a plan to navigate his assignments and helped him late at night after helping his younger brothers to keep him on track. Dantonio had to login on Google Meets for all four of his classes and complete the corresponding work for the day. It was challenging because he'd need help most days and the work was due before the school day was over. Kalob had to login once a day with classwork over multiple apps for the week. He had the most flexibility. I would work with him in between helping Dantonio. Keshawn had two Zoom sessions a day along with coursework for the week. Most days, we were able to complete his assignments quickly. I also had to do physical, occupational, and vison therapy with Keshawn while at home. It was like teaching seven classes online. I was exhausted, especially since each of my boys was in a different grade level, and this was not all I had to do in a day! I feel blessed I was at home for them to stay home. They all maintained either A or A-B averages their 1st grading periods, which made me feel proud of their hard work during such an unpredictable time. Sometimes we don't realize when times are hard for us, they may also be hard for our kids. Take an active interest in your child's mental health by talking to them and spending quality time with them as much as you can. We do so by having family night on Friday's complete with games, movies, and kid food! They look forward to it!

During the pandemic, I cooked every day! This was my one time during the day that wasn't stressful. I could decompress while cooking and listening to music. When the first grading period was over, I sent Keshawn to school with a mask. I felt he needed to do his therapy with his therapist and his classwork at school being special needs. It was all a bit much for me. I sent Kalob and Dantonio to school as well since their school was on the base and under mask mandate. This left Jammieon. He wanted to stay home one more grading period because he'd gotten in the groove with online learning. He returned to school for the third grading period to play basketball. It was amazing to have them all at school again, but each week for the rest of the school year someone was home, whether it be for holidays, newly added teacher planning days, or quarantine. My long-awaited time alone at home when all the kids were in school was thwarted by the COVID pandemic. While I was grateful I was already working from home and able to be there for our kids' needs, it was a very exhausting and trying time where my patience was tested daily!

On the bright side, now that my husband had a stable job and we were in our forever home, I could finally make plans to travel to see friends! All these years, friends have asked me to go places and I have had to say no due to deployments, temporary duty assignments (TDY), pregnancies, and simply being too far away. I know my fellow military spouses can relate. I'd never really traveled while Jamie was active duty except to be in Stephanie's and Berinda's wedding. When we married, we were only stationed on two stateside bases, so I never got to experience life overseas or travel there. I took a road trip with my bestie, Cynthia, to alumni weekend in Linden and attended our 20th high school class reunion in 2018. I traveled to Las Vegas with my bestie, Berinda, for our birthdays in September 2019. I attended Tuskegee's homecoming, for the first time since I graduated, for my twentieth year as a Zeta celebration in 2019. I attended my college roommate, Stephanie's birthday weekend in Atlanta in 2021. I took my first solo trip, for more than a weekend since I've been married, to Dominican Republic in July 2021. I was finally free to get out and travel, see my friends, and reconnect with me. As you can see, I was taking full advantage of all the years I was unable to travel and filling my cup reconnecting with longtime friends.

Since we were here to stay, in January 2020, I decided to reclaim my membership into Zeta Phi Beta Sorority, Incorporated for our Centennial. I'd heard good things about Psi Zeta Chapter in Ft. Worth, TX from my frat brother, Ananias. I told 3 other Sorors Laci, Kenya, and Mineasa in Wichita Falls about my plans and they decided to reclaim as well. While my husband was active duty, we were never near a city that had a chapter and none of the bases we'd been on had one either as some do. In October of 2020, I received an email asking for auditions for Sorors to step in the Macy's Parade. I knew immediately I wanted to audition being a former step mistress but being older I needed a little reassuring first that I still indeed had it. Sometimes, as a military spouse, you lose confidence in yourself or lose yourself and you need a little boost from the people who know and love you. I called two members of my old step team, Brittany and Tiana, and they told me to go for it. I practiced when I could during any free time I had and submitted my tape. Soror Kenya came over and recorded me. I couldn't believe it when I got the news that I made the squad!!! Lesson here is you miss 100% of the chances you don't take in life! It reminded me of the chance I took with Sylvan and where it led. This too was a chance I was glad I took, even though I was initially reluctant! We were to practice on Zoom and fly to New York for taping in November. I was so excited and nervous at the same time. I'd previously been on TV before with Theta Beta Chapter at Spring Bling for BET, but this was the Macy's Parade!!!! Since this was during the pandemic, COVID testing was required before we left and when we arrived. We stayed in the Hyatt near Times Square. We practiced a few times on Zoom and in person once we arrived, but we nailed it! It was an unbelievable, once in a lifetime experience being a part of history as a Centennial Stepper, the first African American sorority of the Divine Nine to perform in the Macy's Parade, and my name will forever be associated with this occasion.

When the application for faculty ranking came out again in October 2020, I was asked to apply again given what had happened with my first application. When I looked at the application, it had been revised. On the first application, I had all the qualifications, but now I wouldn't have some of the qualifications: being on a committee, professional development, and speaking/or reviewing articles. I was told to apply anyway. I submitted what I had, and my application was reviewed and denied. I think Autumn and I had gotten the news at the same time. I asked her if we could talk. I expressed my disappointment and asked her if she would help me get where I needed to be. I told her I'd apply again the following year and if I didn't make it, I'd be leaving NAU. I never had or was assigned a mentor at NAU. After being able to candidly talk to Autumn about all my previous years at NAU during my evaluation, I'd adopted her as mine, whether she knew it or not. She nominated me for a committee and started helping me actively search for professional development. We discussed how the university was not just asking about faculty concerns in the quarterly surveys, but they were making the changes to make things better, offering professional development, training, and faculty meetings to share university business, to name a few. These were all the things I'd need if I were to have a chance at next year's application. At the same time that the university was making changes, Mike, the math faculty lead, was making necessary changes each quarter that streamlined online mathematics instruction for NAU, making life much better. I must say, I am impressed with the math faculty lead, my current supervisor, and the new administration.

When the application was released in 2021, it had been revised yet again. This would be my third and last time around, but I was not discouraged. I knew I'd worked hard the entire year leading up to the application opening, and I'd met all the requirements I had missed before. In the area where speaking engagements or article reviews were the only requirement before, serving in a leadership role for a professional organization was added. This was to my advantage, given I was serving as an advisor for my sorority graduate chapter's undergraduate chapter at Tarleton State. It was exciting to have the qualification and to be able to add this fulfilling work! I'd accepted my nomination by my supervisor to a committee, and I'd taken advantage of every professional development opportunity either sent to me by my supervisor or by the university. I attended the Harold D. Buckingham (HDB) conference put on by NAU, REMOTE: The Connected Faculty Summit, and the Online Learning Consortium (OLC) for professional development, along with faculty development webinars put on by the university and training offered by my sorority and Federally Employed Women. I created an instructional video for one of my courses and sent all contributions I'd made to the committee I was on.

This time, I had all the qualifications. This application would be like night and day compared to the last. I asked my supervisor if she would review all my entries before submission, using her as a resource. After my supervisor reviewed each, I sent my professional development and training, formal appraisal and student feedback, service on academic committees and creation of instructional material, advancement of scholarship by serving in a leadership role for a professional organization, resume, personal statement, verification of total credit hours taught, letter of nomination, and application. I was so proud of myself having completed all the requirements with everything else I had going on. I was also grateful to my supervisor for all her support and help during the process. In February 2022, I found out I'd been promoted from adjunct faculty to assistant professor of mathematics! It took me multiple attempts, but I persevered and was finally successful! I was able to apply the material from my ranking application, along with some ideas for updates for courses from the OLC to my next evaluation in May 2022 and received exceeds expectations across the board for timeliness, engagement, assistance, initiatives, and faculty quality review! This girl was on fire!

In fall 2022, I volunteered to explore a new opportunity teaching in person virtually. I have never had to instruct in person while online. The only time I'd see a student now is during my Zoom office hours, or if a student and I set up a private Zoom tutoring session. I'll have to figure out a way to deliver the content in two 2-hour and 10-minute blocks each week for eight weeks while on Zoom. This will be challenging with the courses being taught in the evening. Evenings can include the kids' extracurricular activities, homework, making dinner, meetings for my organizations, getting everyone ready for bed, and the next day. I am a little terrified, but ready to face the challenge head on, learning as I go, and adding a new skill!

In conclusion, know that you are capable and stronger than you ever thought. Each obstacle that you face and overcome as a military spouse is a testament to that story. No one stays in the storm forever. It can't rain all the time. Don't be afraid to ask for help and use all resources available to you, being open not to overlook any. Keep looking forward to the next day of the rest of your life at all stages of life and strive to make yourself better than you were yesterday.

TAJH-MARIE THOMPSON

CHAPTER NINE

MEET TAJH

hydrant, and others were jumping Double Dutch. The first night was awkward. Where was I going to sleep? Upon arriving, I realized my mother rented a room in the house where she stayed. She shared that bedroom with my little brother, who was around two years old at the time, and his father. I was fifteen years old and there was just no way I was sleeping in the bed with them. My mind was spinning and at that point, I knew I had fucked up and this would become the worst decision I was ever allowed to make in my life. I slept on the couch, with about four other people, for a couple of nights. I awoke every morning as high as a giraffe's ass because they smoked weed 24 hours a day, 7 days a week.

Awaking every morning for three straight years living next door to your mother is not something any fifteen-year-old should have to endure. As the child of a substance abuser, this was my reality. Reflecting back, I see how I made it through. My best friend, Tiff and her family took me in, keeping me out of the house next door that maintained a consistent occupancy of more than fifteen people in five bedrooms.

I have always been compelled by my desire to help others, specifically those who cannot and/or will not help themselves. My path to this career was set early on. In my senior year of high school during my English class, I remember intervening on behalf of one of my classmates. The teacher was pressing him to read and he was not good at it. It felt, to me, that she was intentionally trying to embarrass him. I intervened and was subsequently kicked out of class, given a failing grade, and not allowed to graduate high school on time with the rest of my classmates. My path was set. I am fighting for something greater than myself. My journey to this destination has been a non-traditional but storied one. I spent eight years of my early life in the US Navy, working as a Deck Seaman, Hospital

CHAPTER 9: MEET TAJH

As a child, I was shuffled from pillow to post. While my mother was a great person with a truly remarkable heart, she was unstable. Her addiction to alcohol and drugs severely impaired her ability to be a functional parent. Because of her instability, my two older siblings were sent to live with and be reared by their respective paternal families shortly after their births. Cirrhosis of the liver claimed the life of my father while I was still a young child, so living with him was not a viable option for me. While I did not know how to describe it, I knew that I had suffered a tremendous amount of emotional trauma because of the lack of familial support and the burden of being "different" from everyone else. During my formative years, there was no support or counseling offered to assist me in navigating my emotions. Because I was fortunate enough to mature into a thriving adult, I would like to be able to offer support to others who may face very similar, dire circumstances, and becoming a social worker helped me realize this goal.

My name is Tajh-Marie and I am the mother of seven, a big sister, a city girl, an HBCU graduate, a military veteran, and a military spouse. I was born in Philadelphia, Pennsylvania, where I was raised by my mother. At the age of nine, I moved to the Bronx, New York with my maternal grandparents while my mother was hospitalized and in a coma. When I was approximately thirteen years old, my grandparents retired, and I moved with them to Mt. Gilead, North Carolina. I despised living in the country, and to this day, I still hate the sound of crickets. In the summer of my freshman year in high school, I decided that I no longer wanted to live with my grandparents, and I started to rebel. Shortly after my rebellion they reached their breaking point. They drove me back to Philly, and I had to tu and roll out of the car because they were so ready to drop me off with my moth Arriving in Philly was so exciting. Everyone was sitting outside on their st music was blaring, people were eating crabs, kids were getting wet using the

Corpsman, and Pharmacy Technician. Those years of my military service would prove to be invaluable. The work ethic, attention to detail, dedication, and pursuit of perfection were what set me apart in most positions I held thereafter. I did not, however, master the art of getting up early. I love my sleep. Always have, always will.

I attended Norfolk State University (NSU) and ultimately received my undergraduate degree in psychology. Originally, I was enrolled in NSU's School of Social Work but would be unable to complete any of the internships because I was a single parent and full-time student, maintaining full and part-time employment. Some sage guidance from my academic counselor led me to change my major to psychology.

There are moments in our lives when the going gets tough. When your back is against the wall and you have to make some serious decisions on what is best, right now. My first couple of years in college were an epic struggle. I had grossly underestimated and misunderstood the challenges that lay ahead, all while trying to grasp getting out of the military, being freshly divorced, and being a single parent. My children were both in elementary school, making us all students at the same time. My oldest daughter was born premature and had Asperger's, which made study time with her very long and arduous. The priority focus had to be turned on my children and their education, and then I would have time to focus on myself. Unfortunately, my grades suffered, my patience grew thin, and I barely passed.

My own military career prepared me more than anything for life as a military spouse. The growing pains most experienced as a new military spouse were an afterthought for me. I was already hip to the game. What I was not prepared for was the Officer's spouse's side of the house. When we transferred to Fort Belvoir, Virginia, I joined the Officer's wives' Facebook page, and not long after, they started going off about the Fort Belvoir Community Hospital's pharmacy, for which my husband was responsible. Naturally, I started giving them a piece of my mind. Later, my husband asked me not to engage and get caught up in the drama. It was a little more political than I was accustomed to.

Being a military wife has taught me that marriage is about compromise and communication. I understand that most things are out of our control and that every duty station will not be ideal. I have learned to make the best of every opportunity. When we were stationed in Gulfport, Mississippi, I found a couple of coffee shops that I liked to visit on the weekend. I also found a really good hair salon, chiropractor, masseuse, and nail shop. Self-care is very important to me and it helps to reduce my daily stress, allowing me to take care of my mind and body. In addition to my self-care needs, those shops proved to be hidden gems because I also found friendship and refuge with other military spouses.

One of the greatest challenges associated with being a military wife is ensuring I maintain my own identity and that it is not completely and utterly dependent on my husband, his rank, and his position. When we attend military functions, I feel so out of place, regardless of the fact that I have prior active service. My husband has obtained a higher level of education than I, so naturally, the people he surrounds himself with at these affairs also have a higher level of education. I find myself wanting to scroll through social media to make the time go by, but that would be disrespectful. Sometimes, I am standoffish because we are typically the only couple of color at the dinner table. I often find myself pondering, "how do I fit in here?" Even after receiving my master's degree, this is still a significant challenge for me.

Throughout my life, I have worked several jobs in multiple industries and even started my own business. I have given up as well. I have felt defeated, beaten, and confused about what to do next. I felt guilty when we made the decision for me to be a stay-at-home mom. I felt as though I was not contributing as much as I could have, but my husband was always there to remind me that I contribute just as much as he does. I enjoy being a military wife because I love moving, which could be directly correlated to my childhood and nomad upbringing. I enjoy meeting new people, which affords me the opportunity and ability to adjust well. My husband is my biggest supporter and my hardest critic. He is honest, he is the best father my kids could ever want and does everything in his power to keep me happy, now he just needs to hurry up and retire.

What is it that I hope the reader will take away from this? It is my hope that anyone who reads this gains some insight into the life of a military spouse. The men and women that support those in uniform are a unique breed. They can be called upon at a moment's notice to move to a new city, make new friends, take over mommy and daddy duties, and find new employment.

My tips are as follows:

- Make connections with other military spouses and people in your community.
- Find and learn about the resources available to military families.
- Always have a plan A, B, and C because Murphy's Law is alive and well.
- Do not be afraid or ashamed to ask for and/or to hire help.
- Keep the lines of communication open.
- Even if you consider yourself emotionally stable, you can still benefit from having your own therapist.

www.ingramcontent.com/pod-product-compliance
Lightning Source LLC
Chambersburg PA
CBHW060915190426
43197CB00012BA/2435